cooking with
an asian accent

cooking with an asian accent

EASTERN WISDOM IN A WESTERN KITCHEN

Ying Chang Compestine

Houghton Mifflin Harcourt • Boston • New York • 2014

Cover and interior design by Vertigo Design NYC

Published by Houghton Mifflin Harcourt Publishing Company,
New York, New York.

Published simultaneously in Canada.

For information about permission to reproduce selections from this book,
write to Permissions, Houghton Mifflin Harcourt Publishing Company,
215 Park Avenue South, New York, New York 10003.

ww.hmhco.com

Library of Congress Cataloging-in-Publication Data
Compestine, Ying Chang.
  Cooking with an Asian accent : Eastern wisdom in a Western kitchen /
Ying Chang Compestine.
    p. cm.
  Includes index.
  ISBN 978-1-118-13075-9 (cloth); 978-0-544-18602-6 (ebk.)
1. Cooking, Asian. 2. Cookbooks. lcgft I. Title.
  TX724.5.A1C637 2014
  641.595—dc23
                                2012034911

Printed in the United States of America

DOC 10 9 8 7 6 5 4 3 2 1

To Vinson

May your journey into a new life be happy and successful!

contents

recipes

acknowledgments

Like my journey from Wuhan to California, this book has traveled a long way. I received much inspiration and support from my family, friends, editors, and readers.

A special thanks to my publisher, Natalie Chapman, for your support and flexibility that enabled me to elevate the book to the highest level. Thanks to Brittany Edwards for your enthusiasm and dedication to the book's success.

I am indebted to Edèn Bunchuck and Jacqueline Beach, for your patience and invaluable help. Thanks to Jillian Saland and Christine McKnight for championing this project and your assistance. It has been a great pleasure working with everyone at Houghton Mifflin Harcourt!

Thanks to Dani Fisher for bringing my recipes to life, and to Mariana Velasquez for your exquisite photographs. Thanks to Alison Lew for your tireless effort to create a stunning design for the book.

Thanks to my intern Nicole Price for your help and hard work during oné of the most frantic and exciting times in my career, making it possible for me to juggle many balls at once.

Throughout my writing career, I have always been looking for new ways to save time and make cooking more enjoyable. I'm fortunate to have received assistance and support from the following companies, whose products I've found to be superior: Jenn-Air (luxury kitchen appliances), Calphalon (nonstick and stainless steel cookware), Cuisinart (countertop steam ovens), Vitamix (blenders), Zojirushi American Corporation (rice cookers), and J.A. Henckels International (knives).

Thanks to Beth Hensperger, Margaret Lee, Jill Melton, Regan McMahon and Blair Jackson, Lee and Anne Geiger, Mark and Carol Escajeda, Zora Wan and Kevin Hummel, Zali Lorincz, Chris Krueger, Rich Van Druten, Yshel Lok, and Gerri and Jack Joyce; your friendship enriches my life!

Last but not least, I would like to thank my son, Vinson, my most efficient and intuitive assistant, for chopping, mincing, and marinating. Thanks to my husband, Greg, for your continued support and tireless cooking, cleaning, and tasting.

introduction

On a snowy night in 1984, I stood outside one of the finest restaurants in Beijing. Locals trudged by, oblivious to my presence. As they battled through the northern wind, the corners of their cotton coats flapped like birds' wings. I pulled a red woolen scarf over my head, anxious to carry out my first assignment.

I had recently graduated from Huazhong Normal University in Wuhan, the city of my birth, with a degree in English and American literature. My job as an interpreter for China's National Seismology Bureau required me to travel throughout China to host banquets and conferences, where I would translate for Chinese delegations of government officials, scientists, and foreign geologists.

When the six American geologists finally arrived in a van, escorted by the secret police, I struggled to remove the mittens from my icy-cold hands to greet them. Once inside the heavily carpeted banquet hall, I was embraced by soothing classical Chinese music. Beautifully dressed waitresses immediately brought us jasmine tea. As they filled our cups, the hot tea perfumed the air with a light chrysanthemum fragrance. I held the cup with both hands to warm my stiff fingers. Soon, my appetite was aroused by the aromas of pristinely fresh fish, crisp vegetables, steaming jasmine rice, and simmering spicy noodles heaped on the lazy Susan in the center of our banquet table.

As hungry geologists and chubby government officials enjoyed the meal, I had to stay alert, translating between Chinese and English while fulfilling the duties of a gracious dinner host. At that time, I was not as proficient in English as I am now, and I struggled to translate many of the complex technical phrases, such as levels of damage from the earthquake in Tangshan and data from the satellite stations. Before long, I was glowing with perspiration in my formal wool dress. I felt relief when more dishes arrived and conversation finally slowed—Emperor's Shrimp, savory meatballs, delicate vegetables, flavored rice in bean paste, bean

COOKING WITH AN ASIAN ACCENT

pancakes. Throughout the parade of courses, attentive waitresses continually replenished our small, elegant porcelain bowls with fresh rice or noodles.

In Chinese, the six officials and I expressed bemusement at our foreign guests' style of dining. As soon as the waitress set down a new dish, one of our guests would eagerly pick it up, scoop a portion onto his plate with his fork, and pass it on to the next person.

The director of the Seismology Bureau sitting beside me asked, "Don't they know that they aren't supposed to lift the dishes off the table?"

Thinking of the long government meals I had sat through, I smiled and answered, "It is more efficient than taking small portions with chopsticks."

I was proud of my response, but had no answer to the officials' incredulous remarks when the geologists requested glasses of ice water and cold Tsingtao beer. "Cold drinks on a cold day?" "Why aren't they drinking their warm tea?" "Don't they know about yin-yang balance?"

Even after experiences like this, it was not until I came to the United States that I fully realized how differently our two cultures view food. Asians often see Westerners as unschooled in the concepts of yin-yang balance and food as medicine. They also stereotype Western-style meals as consisting of flavorless vegetables and slabs of meat accompanied by unhealthy cold drinks.

Asian and Western cooking styles differ in that the Western cook expects the diner to do all the work of cutting up ingredients at the table, such as an uncut steak accompanied by a whole baked potato, while the Asian cook does all this in the kitchen. Because of this extra preparation, and what may be unfamiliar ingredients, spices, and cooking equipment, Westerners often shy away from preparing Asian meals at home. Yet modern Westerners are adventurous eaters, eager to try new tastes and flavors.

I am fascinated with food and how it reflects the culture and customs of a country. I have lectured all over the world on healthy eating and living, aboard cruise ships and for various organizations. At every destination, while my fellow tourists marvel at historic landmarks, I search for the best restaurants and local markets. I draw inspiration from these meals, and eagerly incorporate what I've discovered into my new recipes. My cooking has evolved over time to embrace the best of both worlds. Yet, my food, like me, still has a Chinese soul.

For years, Americans have known that Asian cuisine is one of the healthiest in the world. Yet because there is so much mystery surrounding it, I have wanted to demystify it and share my personal evolution of this style of cooking: specifically, incorporating common Western ingredients into Asian cuisine to create something original.

By combining Eastern consciousness with Western efficiency, using readily available nutritious produce, and taking full advantage of a modern time-saving kitchen, you can prepare many delightful and nourishing meals in thirty minutes or less. Whether you are an experienced cook or someone looking for ways to enhance occasional weeknight meals, you will find a wide range of dishes to try in this book. The recipes address the needs of diverse audiences and are cross-indexed for easy reference.

Vegetarians and vegans will find numerous recipes that show just how easy it is to cook satisfying dishes without meat. Most of the recipes in this book are dairy-free, and many dishes that call for meat offer vegetarian alternatives.

Readers can also look up recipes by the appropriate yin-yang balance by season—cooling yin dishes for scorching summers, and energizing yang dishes for the chilly months of winter. Once you are armed with practical knowledge, I hope that you will go beyond these recipes to cook up exciting new dishes that suit your personal tastes and style.

Cooking with an Asian Accent is not another traditional Asian or "quick-meals" cookbook. It's a new cuisine created through my personal East-Meets-West journey, a style of contemporary cooking that addresses the three most important Asian principles: food that is satisfying to the senses, food with yin-yang balance, and food as medicine.

principles of asian cooking

The ancient concept of 阴阳 *yīnyáng*, or yin and yang ☯, originated in China. It describes two interdependent parts that occur within the circle of the universe. The complementary pairing of interdependent opposites makes up all of existence: the sun and the moon, female and male, summer and winter, water and fire, light and dark. It guides many aspects of daily life, from personal relationships to negotiating business; it is also the essence of martial arts and Traditional Chinese Medicine (TCM).

One pillar of TCM is *Shi Liao*, or food therapy: the use of natural foods to promote good health and cure disease. Practitioners of TCM believe that disease arises when the yin-yang properties of the body are no longer in harmony. Lao Tzu, the father of Taoism who lived in the sixth century BC, said, "To see the disease, first look at the diet." He declared that a well-balanced diet is crucial for good health.

Food therapy consists of three important parts: the nature of the food—cooling (yin), warming (yang), and neutral; the nature of the cooking method—steaming (yin), grilling (yang); and a diet suited for each season.

Below I have listed the yin-yang natures of some commonly used ingredients and cooking methods.

INGREDIENTS

cooling	warming	neutral
American ginseng	Beef	Almonds
Apples	Black beans	Beets
Asian pears	Black dates	Broccoli
Asparagus	Black pepper	Brown rice
Bananas	Black rice	Cabbage
Barley	Black sesame	Carrots
Bean sprouts	Brown sugar	Coconut milk
Buckwheat noodles	Black tea	Corn
Cantaloupe	Butter	Eggplant
Celery	Cherries	Eggs
Crabmeat	Chicken	Extra-virgin olive oil
Cucumber	Chiles	Figs
Green onions	Chinese ginseng	Goji berries
Green squash	Cilantro	Grapes
Green tea	Dong quai	Green beans
Honeydew	Duck	Milk
Lemons	Garlic	Oats
Lettuce	Ginger	Olives
Lotus root	Lamb	Oolong or red tea
Moon beans	Leeks	Oyster mushrooms
Mung beans	Mangoes	Oysters
Napa cabbage	Mustard greens	Papayas
Pear	Onions	Peanuts
Peas	Oranges	Plums

cooling	warming	neutral
Radish	Peaches	Pork
Rice noodles	Pineapple	Potatoes
Sesame oil	Pine nuts	Pumpkin
Soybeans	Red meat	Raspberries
Spinach	Shellfish	Red dates
Sugarcane	Shrimp	Sardines
Tangerines	Strawberries	Shiitake mushrooms
Tofu	Toasted nuts	Snow peas
Tomato	Tuna	String beans
Watercress	Vinegar	Sweet potatoes
Watermelon	Walnuts	Trout
White rice	Wine	Whole wheat noodles
White sesame	Yellow squash	Yams

COOKING METHODS

yin	yang
Blanching	Deep-frying
Boiling	Grilling
Poaching	Roasting
Steaming	Stir-frying

It is believed that yang foods such as red meats and fatty foods increase the body's metabolism, raising the internal temperature, while yin foods such as leafy vegetables and succulent fruits lower the metabolism and cool the body.

A person who consumes an excessive amount of yang foods might produce a surplus of energy, becoming hot-tempered and aggressive. It will lead to restless and agitated sensations and may result in acne and halitosis. Meanwhile, a person who consumes too many yin foods might feel fatigued and chilled due to lack of energy, resulting in sluggish behavior, depression, or lethargy.

While the concept of food as medicine is new to many Westerners, modern science has, in fact, confirmed this traditional Eastern belief, and has even coined a new word for this concept: nutraceuticals.

For TCM doctors, there is no strict boundary between everyday food and food prescribed as medicine. For example ginger, garlic, and turmeric, common spices in Asian cooking, are considered warming and often used as stomach tonics and for combating bacterial infections. Other common foods such as soy, cucumber, and daikon are considered cooling and used in the treatment of fevers, headaches, and skin rashes due to excess heat in the body.

My mother taught me at a young age that "no expensive medicine is as good as simple, natural food." Instead of reaching for pills to remedy small discomforts, such as fatigue, an upset stomach, or a skin blemish, she told me to interpret those symptoms as a sign that my diet needs rebalancing and my mind and body require rest.

Researchers believe that the low rates of certain types of diseases in Asia are due to a diet rich in many healthy ingredients such as garlic, which helps protect against stomach cancer and heart disease; ginger, which lowers cholesterol; soy, which eases menopausal symptoms; shiitake mushrooms, which have antioxidant and anticancer benefits; ginseng, which stimulates the immune system and improves both mental and physical performance; and green tea, which inhibits the production of carcinogens and promotes weight loss.

Today, in the West, the *Tao Te Ching* is one of the most-studied books of Chinese philosophy. *Tao* in Chinese means "the path" or "the way." For more than four thousand years, people have followed these teachings, with their strong emphasis on simplicity in every aspect of life, including food. Chapter 12 of the *Tao Te Ching* states:

> The five colors make one blind in the eyes
>
> The five sounds make one deaf in the ears
>
> The five flavors make one tasteless in the mouth

According to Taoist principles, one should enjoy simple foods with a limited number of flavors, so as to not overwhelm the mouth. Yet in our modern times, we also have to make a conscious decision to avoid processed fast foods that are oversaturated with artificial sweeteners, sodium, and fats. These foods have been robbed of their original taste and nutritional value, which translates into the alarming growth of chronic diseases such as heart disorders, diabetes, obesity, asthma, and food allergies that now plague our youngest generation. As the Western adage goes, "You are what you eat."

The concept of food as medicine comes from a time when people lived closer to nature and had to handle its changes directly. Our insulated, modern lifestyle isolates us from the seasons almost as much as from the origins of our food. Yet each change of season has a profound effect on us. Whether its spring's hay fever, the colds brought on by viruses rampant in winter, or fatigue from summer heat, the ancient wisdom of TCM turns to food to help the body cope with and heal from these stresses.

Simple, plant-based foods are the key for maintaining our internal balance of yin and yang, and they help us achieve fulfillment in life. The closer food is to its natural state, and the less processed and refined, the more nourishment it contains.

The yin and yang principles in each of the four seasons are explained on the following pages as a framework for the holistic benefits of **food as medicine**.

SPRING

As a popular Chinese saying goes, "Spring comes, and hundreds of flowers blossom." As the returning warmth awakens nature, yang forces are on the rise along with the temperature. High humidity and damp air heralds outbursts of bacteria, viruses, insects, and pollen.

Spring foods should focus on prevention and cleansing. Take precautions against colds, the flu, and sinus congestion. Consume plenty of herbs and seasonal vegetables, such as soy, and seafood that are rich in antioxidants, vitamins, and fiber to clear out toxins accumulated over the long winter.

Try recipes such as Tomato and Crabmeat Egg Drop Soup (page 67), Mango-Lobster Spring Rolls (page 112), Stir-Fried Bok Choy with Shiitake Mushrooms (page 132), Pearl Meatballs (page 208), Tofu Filled with Crabmeat and Pork (page 193), and Rice Pudding with Almonds and Coconut (page 239).

SUMMER

The summer solstice lands in the fifth month of the Chinese lunar calendar, or June on the Western calendar. Practitioners of TCM believe that summer's sweltering heat and humidity lead to fatigue, loss of appetite, and dizziness, making it important to eat cooling yin foods. Vibrant salads of leafy vegetables and juicy sweet fruits, fish, and cool beverages are preferable to the heavy yang foods favored in wintertime.

This is the season to eat less and drink more. At the height of summer, TCM also advises that foods be flavored with pungent spices to help stimulate the appetite and harmonize the differences between inner and outer temperatures.

Try The Empress's Secret Beauty Soup (page 56), Tofu and Cashew Lettuce Cups (page 124), Snow Pea and Crabmeat Salad (page 86), Chickpea-Avocado Salad with Spicy Sesame Sauce (page 89), Steamed Fish with Spicy Ginger Sauce (page 206), and Summer Fruit Refresher (page 221).

FALL

Fall is the season when yang begins to fade as yin becomes more prominent. The season's dry winds deplete the body's fluids, contributing to coughs, sore throats, and thirst—symptoms often associated with the common cold. TCM doctors suggest eating foods that combat this seasonal dryness, lubricate the digestive system, and strengthen the inner vital forces.

This is the season to fortify the body's energies before winter sets in. Tofu, a food cherished during the fall season, helps regulate body heat and reduce seasonal dryness. My mother, a TCM doctor, often served tofu to me and my brothers when we suffered from fevers and coughs. Other ingredients such as daikon and juicy pears are known for their medicinal properties and combat dryness, moisturize the lungs, and relieve asthma and constipation.

Try Nourishing Ribs with Goji Berries and Red Dates (page 57), Almond Trout with Mango-Ginger Salsa (page 175), Turmeric Scallops with Turnips and Cashews (page 144), Sautéed Kale with Cashews and Raisins (page 137), Brown Rice Stir-Fry with Flavored Tofu and Vegetables (page 147), and Steamed Asian Pears with Rock Sugar (page 232).

WINTER

Winter is the season when we need to strengthen our bodies' yang to combat seasonal chills and keep us warm within. Therefore, TCM doctors strongly oppose drinking chilled beverages or ice water, or consuming cooling foods such as watermelons, cucumbers, or ice cream. They believe that such foods inhibit the appetite, slow down the metabolism, damage the digestive system, and hamper steady blood flow, which can lead to chronic pain and disease.

Winter foods should be filled with warmth and energy. Good choices for this season are foods rich in nutrients, high in protein, and flavored with pungent warm spices or cooked with energizing herbs.

Try Lamb, Potato, and Carrot Stew (page 70), Garlic-Pecan Chicken (page 141), Lion's Head Meatballs in Lettuce Leaves (page 122), Forbidden Rice with Eggs and Almonds (page 148), Coconut-Curry Shrimp and Rice (page 205), and Banana Bread Pudding with Vanilla-Rum-Chocolate Sauce (page 237).

east meets west pantry

My pantry and refrigerator are much like my life, a medley of influences from both the East and the West.

I fill them with the best ingredients of both worlds. I use whole wheat tortillas to replace traditional Chinese wrappers and healthy extra-virgin olive oil for stir-frying instead of traditional corn, vegetable, or soybean oils used in Asian cooking.

Thanks to the widespread interest in international cuisine, I can easily find all of my ingredients at my local supermarkets and farmers' markets. Now, you can even order fresh produce and have it delivered to your door.

As a Chinese saying goes, "The best cook can't make a meal without ingredients." It's important to keep a well-stocked pantry, which will save you time and make cooking a healthy meal easy and fun.

fresh ingredients

baby bok choy. Baby bok choy has dark green leaves and a thick white stem 6 to 8 inches long. It is a smaller, young version of bok choy that tastes sweeter and is less fibrous. When buying, choose bok choy with tightly closed packed buds. Avoid any with yellow leaves or stems. Baby bok choy is available year-round and is best stored in a refrigerator's crisper bin, where it will remain fresh for up to 4 days. Use baby bok choy in stir-fries for a burst of green, or add to soups.

chiles. Chiles come in many varieties and vary greatly in terms of heat. Choose them based on how spicy you like your food. Look for fresh chiles free of brown patches or black spots. Wear gloves when preparing very hot chiles. After handling, don't touch your eyes, lips, or other sensitive areas. Wash your hands, knives, and cutting board thoroughly with soapy water. The chiles I use include the medium-hot jalapeño, which is shiny green and turns red when ripe; the Fresno, a California-grown chile, which resembles the jalapeño, but is slightly broader, about 2 inches long and 1 inch wide; and the very hot serrano, a slender chile that can be green, red, or yellow.

daikon. Also known as Oriental or Japanese radish, it has a sweet, peppery taste and is shaped like an oversized white carrot. Look for daikon that are firm and have bright, smooth skins. It is commonly used in Asian soups, salads, and stir-fries. It can last for weeks stored in a paper bag in a cool, dry place. Daikon is low in calories and high in vitamin C, and is considered a cooling food in TCM.

dried black dates. Black dates, which look a bit like prunes, have a smoky fragrance. Dried black dates are about ¾ inch long and ½ inch in diameter with a small pit inside. Available in Asian supermarkets and herb shops, they are often combined with dong quai and ginseng. Black dates are considered good for PMS and for regulating the symptoms of menopause.

edamame. When harvested, edamame, or soybeans, are green and sweet with a very mild taste. Packed with nutrition, soybeans are made into tofu, soybean oil, soy milk, soy sauce, miso, and much more. Edamame can be found in the frozen section of health food stores, supermarkets, and Asian markets. They are packaged shelled or in the pod. Sometimes you can even find fresh ones at farmers' markets. Edamame in the pod makes a great snack or a delightful appetizer. Boil in lightly salted water for 8 to 10 minutes. Shelled beans can be cooked with other ingredients in stir-fried dishes or soups.

mushrooms. I use various types of mushrooms, including shiitake, maitake, and oyster mushrooms. They are bursting with delicious flavor and are loaded with valuable medicinal properties. When buying fresh mushrooms, look for those with firm, dry flesh that is free of blemishes. Buy the amount you know you'll use in a few days, as mushrooms stored for too long in the refrigerator will become slimy. To help offset this, place them in a paper bag or wrap them in dry paper towels and store in the refrigerator. Rinse the caps under cold water to remove dirt and sand just before using. Squeeze the mushrooms in your hand to wring out the water thoroughly. Reserve the knobby and woody stems for stocks, soups, or stews. Feel free to substitute one variety for another within recipes.

> **shiitake mushrooms.** East Asians have prized shiitakes' taste and reputed medicinal benefits for more than two thousand years. Considered a neutral food, shiitakes are prescribed for a variety of ailments ranging from cancer prevention and treatment, fatigue, arthritis, and colds, to gastrointestinal problems, liver ailments, and vision problems. Both fresh and dried shiitakes are available on the market. Fresh shiitakes should be

stored and prepared as described on the previous page for mushrooms. Dried shiitakes come in different grades. Look for mushrooms with thick caps. They will keep for up to 6 months if stored in a cool, dark place. Dried shiitakes need to be rehydrated; soak the mushrooms in hot water until soft, for about 15 minutes. (The soaking time will vary with type and size.) Rinse the gills under running water to clean them of any dirt or sand. Squeeze the mushrooms in your hand to wring out the water thoroughly.

soybean sprouts. The crisp sprouts of germinated soybeans are an excellent source of nutrition since they are high in protein and packed with vitamin C. Soybean sprouts can be found in Asian markets and natural food stores. They must be cooked quickly over low heat or they will get mushy. They are also ideal for salads, soups, and stir-fries.

tofu and tofu-based products. Tofu is a soft food, the consistency of cheese, made by curdling fresh hot soy milk with a coagulant. Tofu is a bland product that easily absorbs the flavors of other ingredients when cooked. It is rich in high-quality proteins and B-vitamins, and low in sodium.

fresh tofu. Fresh tofu comes in three different varieties: extra-firm, firm, and soft. Each type is also available in low-fat varieties. You can find them in the refrigerator section of most supermarkets, where they are usually sold as 16-ounce blocks packed in water-filled plastic tubs. Firm tofu is dense and solid. It can be cubed and added to soups, or stir-fried, or grilled. Firm tofu is higher in protein, fat, and calcium than other forms of tofu. Soft tofu is good for recipes that call for blending the tofu.

silken tofu. Silken tofu is not the same as fresh tofu. It is creamy and can be used as a replacement for sour cream in many dip recipes. Packaged in a rectangular aseptic cardboard container, silken tofu doesn't need re-frigeration, giving it a long shelf life. With its custard-like consistency, it can be used in salad dressings, desserts, and soups. It is available in soft, firm, and extra-firm, and light and low-fat varieties.

flavor-baked tofu. Flavor-baked tofu, brownish in color, is made by pressing water out of fresh tofu, marinating it in seasonings, and baking it. Brownish in color, it is an ideal meat substitute in stir-fried dishes and tossed into salads. I like the WhiteWave brand, available in five flavors.

herbs, spices, and seasonings

chile garlic paste. Made from red or green chiles, garlic, salt, and other seasonings, chile garlic paste is sold in jars. Look for a brand that is low in sodium and does not contain MSG. Refrigerate after opening.

cilantro. Also called Chinese parsley or fresh coriander, cilantro leaves have a uniquely fragrant, slightly musky flavor. Choose bunches with thin stems and avoid any with yellow, wilted leaves. Store cilantro in the refrigerator for up to 6 days. This herb is a flavorful addition to a variety of dishes and is often used in sauces or as a garnish for noodles. When flavoring stocks or soups, use both leaves and stalks, but discard the stalks before serving.

curry powder. This powdered ground spice mix is a combination of cumin, coriander, turmeric, and cinnamon, while curry paste is a combination of oils and curry spices. Curry has a variety of flavors and varying levels of spiciness. Red curry contains red chiles while green curry contains green chiles. Yellow curry contains a blend of dried spices. Try them all and find the types that fit your taste. I prefer using curry powder because I can easily adjust the flavor when cooking, and some curry pastes are also high in sodium and saturated fats. Curry has a very strong flavor, so in this case, less is more.

dong quai. Also known as *Angelica sinensis*, dong quai is a Chinese herb for women. According to Chinese doctors, dong quai has phytoestrogens, which account for its ability to ease menopausal symptoms and help blood circulation. Donq quai is sold in three forms—knobs, slices, and pills. Knobs have an ivory color with brown veins and are usually 1 inch long and 3 inches in diameter. Like ginseng roots, they require a long cooking time. Knobs weigh about 1 ounce each. When refrigerated in an airtight jar, dong quai can last 8 to 12 months. Slices are about ⅛ inch thick and 3 or 4 inches around. You can buy dong quai at Chinese medicine shops or order it online. Some health food stores even carry it.

five-spice powder. Also known as five-flavor powder, five-spice powder is a mixture of star anise, Szechuan peppercorns, fennel, cloves, and cinnamon. Five-spice powder has a pungent, fragrant, spicy, and sweet taste. It has a long shelf life when kept in a tightly sealed jar.

garlic. A member of the onion family, garlic is one of the essential spices of Asian cooking. TCM categorizes garlic as a yang food, with important medicinal properties. And Western science acknowledges that garlic contains many active compounds believed to prevent and treat a number of illnesses by stimulating immune function and fighting viruses, such as those that cause colds and flu. It also has antibacterial components that kill germs in food and keep our digestive system healthy. In some northern regions of China, many people eat raw garlic with practically every meal. When purchasing fresh garlic, pick out bulbs that are large and feel firm. Look for those that are tight, unbroken, and free of any soft spots. To prepare garlic, place the cloves on a cutting board. Holding a chef's knife flat over the garlic, apply light pressure on the flat of the blade with your hand, slightly crushing the clove. The skin will crack open and peel off with ease. Garlic should be stored in a cool, dark place. Unbroken bulbs will normally last for a few months, while individual cloves will only last a few weeks or less. You shouldn't store garlic in the refrigerator or freezer, where it will absorb moisture and lose its fresh flavor and sharp tang.

varieties of garlic. Garlic's botanical name is *Allium sativum*. It belongs to the *Allium* genus, a family which includes onions, chives, and leeks. A garlic plant will grow from a clove to about 6 inches high, with spearlike stalks. A head of garlic consists of eight to twenty cloves clustered together in a bulb, and a knot of thin roots at the foot. There are two general varieties of garlic: hardneck and softneck. Hardneck garlic has a little stick in the middle (hence the name). It is more difficult to grow, and more perishable. However, hardneck varieties offer a wider range of flavor, and their skin is more colorful. Hardneck garlic is believed to be more closely related to wild garlic. Widely available in supermarkets, softneck garlic varieties contain no hard stick in the center. They are easier to grow and offer the longest shelf life. Their skin is usually white or silvery. Since the stalk is pliable, softneck varieties are used to make garlic braids. Elephant garlic is actually a type of leek, and not true garlic; it has a very mild flavor.

ginger. Another vital spice in Asian cooking is fresh ginger. It brings out the flavors of vegetables, and it also removes fishy and raw odors from seafood and meat while enhancing their taste. In the yin-yang concept, ginger is considered yang and warming. It is used in TCM for treating nausea, stomach problems, colds, joint pain, and frostbite. Ginger ranges from the mild young gingers with pale, tender skin, to the pungent and fiery mature gingers with thick, flaky skin that will suck your breath away. Look for ginger that is plump, firm, and not too fibrous. Avoid ginger with wrinkles or that feels light, as it indicates that it has dried out, robbing it of most of its beneficial properties and flavor. Peeling ginger is optional, especially with young ginger, which has soft and tender skin. I prefer to leave the skin on to fully benefit from its medicinal value and appreciate its taste and fragrance. Fresh ginger will keep for several weeks if it's kept dry and cool. For extended storage, wrap ginger in a dry paper towel or keep it in a brown paper bag, stored in the vegetable crisper in your refrigerator. Or you can store ginger the way the Chinese do, by burying it in your rice jar.

ginseng. Due to the way the shape of the ginseng root often resembles a humanlike figure, it is called *ren shen* in Chinese, meaning "root of person." Ginseng plays a major role in the TCM concept of yin and yang. When one's balance is disturbed, a suitable type of ginseng is administered, often by being cooked with food. Ginseng comes in the form of either fresh or dried whole roots, or minced or powdered dry roots, as well as fresh or dry slices. It can be purchased at Chinese medicine shops, health food stores, and online. For cooking, I have found that ginseng tea and dried slices are most convenient for soups or stews. Asian ginseng is native primarily to China and Korea, and has a sweet, mild taste. It is considered yang and warm. Therefore it stimulates and boosts energy and vitality. It is often served during winter, in soups, stews, and beverages, to the elderly, infirm, new mothers, postmenopausal women, and vegetarians. However, due to its yang properties, it is to be avoided during the summer and not served to those suffering from the flu or fevers.

american ginseng. American ginseng was discovered by Jesuit missionaries in the 1700s and 1800s, growing wild in the northern United States. It is most commonly found in Wisconsin and Canada. Having a yin effect, it is used to treat fevers, menopause, hyperactivity, and what Chinese herbal doctors call "yin-deficient ailments." Due to its mild, cooling effect, American ginseng is used during most of the year, especially during the summer months.

siberian ginseng. Siberian ginseng grows mainly in the northern, tundra regions of eastern Russia. Technically, it is not a ginseng but has similar properties to true ginseng. Siberian ginseng is considered neutral and is believed to increase energy and stamina and support a weak heart and lungs. When Asian ginseng became expensive and hard to find, Russians used the Siberian version as an alternative. Its root requires days of soaking and cooking due to the tough fibers, but it is widely used by athletes and performers in Russia. Siberian ginseng can be used year-round. It has a smoky, sweet taste.

goji berries. Also known as wolfberries, the name is derived from the pinyin spelling *gŏuqĭ*. Goji berries have a sweet taste and resemble ½-inch-long, orange-red raisins. They ripen from July to October. High in iron and calcium, goji berries have long played an important role in TCM. They are believed to improve eyesight and circulation, protect the liver, boost sperm production, and enhance the immune system. In TCM, goji berries are considered neutral in their nature, strengthening the liver, lungs, and kidneys while enriching yin. They are eaten raw, cooked in soup, sprinkled over salads, consumed in a juice or wine, or brewed in an herbal tea. You can buy dried goji berries at health food stores or herbal shops.

lemongrass. A slender green stalk up to 3 feet long, lemongrass is commonly used in Southeast Asian cooking. It has a woody texture and a delicate lemon aroma and flavor. It's often used in broths and sauces and should be discarded before serving. Use only the 5- to 7-inch bulblike base. Peel and discard the external tough, dry leaves. Shredded bulbs are used to flavor soups while minced bulbs are used in sauces. You can find lemongrass in Asian markets or in the produce department of well-stocked supermarkets. Lemon peels can be used as a substitute.

miso. This salty fermented paste is made from soybeans and grains, such as rice or barley, and then aged in cedar vats for one to three years. White miso, made with rice, has a sweet, delicate flavor, while red miso, made with barley, is saltier and has a stronger flavor. I often keep both types in my fridge. Miso can be used to flavor a variety of foods, such as soups, sauces, dressings, and marinades. Store miso in the refrigerator, where it will keep for several months. A little bit of it goes a long way.

rock sugar. This amber-colored crystallized sugar comes in big or small chunks. To break up a large piece, wrap it in a kitchen towel, place it on a hard surface, and hit it with a hammer. Rock sugar is available in Asian grocery stores, sold in plastic bags. Store it in an airtight glass jar in a cool, dry place and it will last for up to 12 months. It is most commonly used in Asian desserts.

turmeric. A relative of ginger, turmeric is a perennial plant that grows 3 to 5 feet tall. The turmeric root, or rhizome, is tuberous, with rough, yellowish brown skin and a dull orange interior that turns bright yellow when dried and powdered. Turmeric is considered warm and therefore yang. It has long been used in traditional Chinese medicines as a stomach tonic and blood purifier, as well as for a variety of skin conditions and liver problems. Fresh and dry turmeric can be used in stews, stir-fried dishes, or marinades. It has a bitter, sharp taste. It is also widely used as a natural food coloring. When looking for fresh turmeric, select roots that are plump and hard. Wrap fresh turmeric root with a paper towel and place in a sealed bag. It will keep for several weeks. Powdered turmeric is ground from dried turmeric. It is sold by itself or mixed with other spices. Since it has a long shelf life, look for a product in a tightly sealed glass container so it will not lose its flavor over time.

dry ingredients

black pepper. Black pepper comes from ground peppercorns, the dried fruit of the black pepper plant, and is most commonly used as a spice and seasoning. I have found that it tastes best freshly ground, but store-bought, preground black pepper will work in a pinch. Black pepper is an anti-inflammatory agent that also serves as a good source of manganese, iron, potassium, vitamin C, vitamin K, and dietary fiber. Aiding in digestion, black pepper is an excellent ingredient for preventing diarrhea, constipation, and colic. Since everyone has different tastes, experiment and find which amount is best for you! Remember, always start with a little less than you think you need, and go from there. In most recipes, I suggest seasoning to taste. A good starting point is ¼ teaspoon for a dish serving four.

flour tortillas. Typically made with refined flour, healthy whole wheat varieties are becoming increasingly available in supermarkets. Sizes of tortillas range from 6 to 10 inches in diameter. Heat (see "Two Easy Ways to Heat Tortillas," page 119) to make them soft and pliable for wrapping around fillings. I recommend whole wheat flour tortillas over corn tortillas for these recipes. (To make your own tortillas, see the recipe on page 118.) I use them in place of traditional Chinese homemade wrappers because they are readily available, healthy, and a tasty time-saver.

noodles. While each recipe calls for a specific type of noodle, you can substitute any of those listed below. Dry bean and rice noodles must be soaked before cooking. Do not soak soba or wheat noodles. Angel hair pasta or linguine may be substituted for thin bean and rice noodles; use fettuccine in place of wide rice noodles. When buying noodles, check the nutrition label and buy noodles that are low in sodium.

> **bean threads.** These fine white noodles are made from ground mung beans and come in various lengths and thicknesses. They are sold in neat bundles in plastic packages. They will keep in a dry, tightly sealed container for up to 6 months. They are popular in soups, cold noodle dishes, and fillings.

> **rice noodles.** Made from long-grain rice flour, these white noodles come in a variety of shapes and thicknesses. Refrigerate fresh ones and cook within a couple of days. Keep the dry form in a tightly sealed container in a cool, dry place for up to 6 months. Rice noodles are popular in stir-fries, cold noodle dishes, and soups.

> **soba noodles.** Made from a blend of buckwheat and wheat flours, these Japanese noodles also come in flavored varieties, including green tea, vegetables such as spinach or carrots, or wild yam.

> **udon noodles.** These Japanese noodles made with wheat flour and water are ideal for soups and stir-fried dishes.

> **wheat noodles.** Made from white flour, water, and sometimes eggs, these noodles are sold fresh or dry and come in various shapes.

nori. Best known for wrapping sushi rolls, nori is available in Asian markets and natural food stores. This popular and nutritious form of seaweed is roasted and formed into thin sheets. It can also be shredded and used to garnish soups and Japanese-style dishes.

nuts. Chinese medicine believes all nuts have mind-strengthening qualities and increase virility. Walnuts, pecans, and peanuts, which calm the kidneys and warm the lungs, are most commonly used. Nuts can be included in salads and stir-fries as healthy sources of protein and flavor or as garnishes to provide a crisp texture. They can also be eaten as simple, healthy snacks, or in dessert soups. Nuts can last for weeks if properly stored dry in an airtight container.

rice. As a staple, rice dates back to the Chou period (1122–256 BC). Over the centuries, rice has shaped the culture of Asia. It is viewed as a grain that links heaven and earth. Festivals and traditions evolved around the planting and harvesting of the rice crop. For many Asians, life without rice is simply unthinkable. Rice is highly regarded in Asia for its nutritional and medicinal value. It is believed to tone the body, strengthen the spleen, clear out heat, and provide yin-yang balance in the body.

long-grain rice. These long, slender grains are each about four times as long as they are wide. It's the favored rice in China. When cooked, the rice separates easily and is less starchy than short grain. When leftover and chilled, it is perfect for making fried rice dishes.

short-grain rice. Round, plump, oval grains are preferred in eastern Asia. High in starch, the rice sticks together when cooked. It is used as an accompaniment to main dishes, for Japanese sushi, and in Chinese congee (a rice soup).

glutinous rice. Also known as sweet or sticky rice, it is a variety of short-grain, with a short, round, pearl-like form. High in starch, when cooked it turns translucent, soft, and sticky. It is widely used in Asian festival dishes and desserts.

black rice. Also called Forbidden Rice. Chinese legend tells us that originally only the Emperor was allowed to eat this exotic grain. It has a deep purple color, a delicious nutty taste, and a soft texture. Rich in iron and considered a blood toner by Chinese medicine doctors, it's available at natural food stores and Asian markets.

sweet brown rice. This is a type of short-grain rice. You can find it in the bulk sections of health food stores, or in Asian grocery stores. It contains more fiber than white rice. I use it in stir-fry recipes like Brown Rice Stir-Fry with Flavored Tofu and Vegetables (page 147), and as a side dish for many recipes that would traditionally be served with white rice.

sweet rice flour. This flour is made from glutinous rice and is widely used in Asian desserts. It is much stickier than rice flour made from long-grain rice. Asian and some natural food stores carry it in small plastic packages.

wild rice. Not really rice at all, it is a seed of an aquatic grass that grows wild in the Great Lakes area of the United States. It's low in fat, high in B vitamins, and rich in protein. Wild rice has a chewy texture and nutty flavor.

rice paper wrappers. These round or triangular translucent sheets made from rice flour are widely used in Vietnamese and Thai cooking. To use, dip a wrapper in warm water for a few seconds; the delicate sheets become soft and pliable. Once the package is opened, store the wrappers in airtight plastic bags. If stored in a cool, dry place, they will last a couple of months. You can find them at most Asian markets and specialty stores.

salt/sea salt. Sea salt is a superior choice to the iodized salt available in the market. It contains many trace minerals that our body needs, including potassium, which is essential for helping muscles to function properly and prevents muscle pains, spasms and cramps. When using salt, keep in mind less is better. It also depends on the season—on a hot summer day you might want to add more to your soup than in the winter dish. Since everyone has different tastes, in many of the recipes I list the salt to taste. As a guide, start with ⅛ teaspoon for a dish serving four and add more if needed.

wonton wrappers. Made from wheat flour, water, and sometimes eggs, wonton wrappers come in two varieties. The thicker, round wonton wrappers are also called gyoza. These thick skins are ideal for pan-fried pot stickers, or boiled Asian dumplings used in soups. They can also be used for steamed dumplings. The square, thin-skinned wonton wrappers are often deep-fried or used for steamed dumplings. Both kinds will keep, well wrapped, in the refrigerator for up to 1 week or for up to 3 months in the freezer. Find them at most grocery stores in the Asian produce section and at Asian markets. Keep wrappers in a bag at all times to retain their moisture. When cooking with the wrappers, take out only one at a time. Leave the rest in the bag, covered with a damp cloth to prevent them from drying out.

liquid ingredients

canola oil. Rich in monounsaturated fats and low in saturated fats, canola oil also contains a good amount of linolenic acid, an essential omega-3 fatty acid.

Canola oil's mild, bland taste makes it a good, all-purpose cooking oil that won't interfere with other flavors.

coconut milk. Made from the milky white meat of mature coconuts, coconut milk has a rich, mildly sweet flavor. Coconut milk's richness comes from the high sugar and oil content, which is why I prefer using reduced-fat brands. I often dilute it by half with rice or soy milk. When recipes call for coconut milk, you can use the canned unsweetened variety. The thick cream tends to float on top. Make sure to mix it well before using. Store leftover coconut milk in a sealed container in the freezer. It will last for a few months.

fish sauce. This thin, clear brown sauce is made from fermented shrimp or fish and has a very fishy odor and salty taste. The fishy smell greatly diminishes with cooking. In Southeast Asia and southern China, fish sauce is a popular way to salt food. Flavors vary in saltiness and aroma. The salty version is often used for flavoring stir-fries, while the sweet-and-sour version is commonly used for dipping. Fish sauce is sold in bottles in most supermarkets, health food stores, and Asian specialty markets. It will keep for several months without refrigeration.

olive oil. Although it is not an Asian ingredient, I have used olive oil for years as a cooking oil because of its health benefits. It is rich in monounsaturated fats and low in saturated fats. It comes in several varieties, from rich-tasting, extra-virgin oil of the first cold pressing, to refined oil that is bland in taste and used for general cooking. Use extra-virgin oil when the taste of the oil is important, such as in some salad dressings. Some olive oil is labeled "light," meaning it is light in taste, not calories.

rice vinegar. Made from rice, it has a less acidic taste than cider or wine vinegar. Rice vinegar comes in black, red, and yellow varieties. Black rice vinegar is dark in color and strong in taste; red vinegar is sweet and spicy in taste; and yellow is very mild. There are also varieties of rice vinegars on the market that are flavored with seasonings such as garlic, basil, and chiles. In a pinch, you can substitute balsamic for black vinegar; cider vinegar for red and yellow.

rice wine. Made by fermenting glutinous rice, yeast, and spring water, rice wine has a rich, mellow taste that is slightly sweet. It is often used to flavor seafood and meats. You can substitute dry sherry.

sesame oil. Made from toasted sesame seeds, sesame oil has a strong nutty flavor and aroma. A few teaspoons of sesame oil add a distinctive taste to many dishes. The darker the oil, the stronger the flavor. Since it heats rapidly and the flavor evaporates quickly, it should not be used as a cooking oil but added at the end of cooking or mixed into a sauce.

soy milk or soy beverages. Made from ground soybeans and water, these thick beverages are a good alternative for those who are lactose intolerant, allergic to dairy, or want to reduce their fat intake and increase the amount of soy in their diets.

Soy beverages come in many different flavors. They are sold mostly in aseptic containers (nonrefrigerated and shelf stable) and in quart or half-gallon containers in the dairy case. In recipes, soy milk can be substituted for cow's milk cup for cup. Reduce the fat content in recipes that call for coconut milk by replacing half the coconut milk with soy milk. Look for a brand low in sugar.

soy sauce. Made from fermented soybeans, water, salt, and sometimes wheat, soy sauce comes in two main types, light and dark. Dark soy sauce is thicker and tastes stronger than light soy sauce. It is used for flavor and to add color to dishes. The light sauce is used in dipping sauces. I like naturally fermented soy sauces that are made from organic soybeans and that are low in sodium. You can find them at natural food stores and in the Asian section of many supermarkets. To reduce the sodium in regular soy sauce, replace half of the soy sauce called for in the recipe with lemon juice, rice vinegar, or water. Soy sauce will keep for several months without refrigeration.

Shoyu is a type of soy sauce made from a blend of soybeans and wheat. Tamari is made only from soybeans, a by-product of making miso. It is ideal for those who have a gluten intolerance. Teriyaki is similar to soy sauce, but has additional ingredients such as pineapple juice, chile, ginger, garlic, or sugar. It has a savory, sweet flavor and works well as a marinade. Always look for a brand that is made with natural ingredients.

soy yogurt. Made from soy milk, soy yogurt has a creamy texture, making it ideal for smoothies and desserts. Soy yogurt comes in a variety of flavors. Look for a brand low in sugar.

tea. All teas come from the *Camellia sinensis* plant. Different processes produce three major types of tea. Fully fermented leaves result in black tea, considered yang, or warming. Green tea, made from unfermented leaves, is considered yin, or cooling. Oolong, or red tea, is partially fermented and has a flavor and color that falls between black tea and green tea. It is characterized as neutral. Tea is a well-known source of antioxidants, vital for cardiovascular health.

The Chinese have been cooking with tea for nearly as long as they have been drinking it, since about 800 AD. Tea sauces are used for marinades, cooking, and dipping. For stir-fries and sautés, dry tea leaves are added to flavor the oil before other ingredients are added. The delicious aroma of tea gives the food a unique, refreshingly natural flavor. When using the tea from tea bags for seasoning, snip open the tea bags, remove the contents, and discard the empty bags.

brewing and cooking with tea

I SAW MY GRANDMOTHER COOK WITH TEA when I was young. She used the dry leaves as a seasoning, the brew as a sauce base, and the infused leaves as vegetables. Her favorite teas were Dragon Well and gunpowder. Below are a few simple steps to follow when brewing or cooking with tea.

Use filtered water to brew tea when possible. The chemicals and minerals in tap water alter the flavor of the tea.

Never boil water for tea in an aluminum teakettle, or steep tea in plastic or aluminum. Use stainless steel teakettles, which are nonreactive and don't absorb flavors or odors, thus providing the purest water for tea.

For white and green teas: Brew at temperatures that are 160° to 170°F (71° to 76°C) for at least 3 to 4 minutes to receive the full health benefits; this is when the water first begins to stir.

For black tea: Brew at near boiling temperature, 195°F (91°C); this is when the water is dancing and hissing.

cooking with tea

- When using tea for sauces or soup bases, use two to three times as much tea as you would for drinking.

- When using tea as a seasoning, add the dry leaves to the heated oil like any other seasoning.

- When a recipe calls for loose tea, you can also substitute the contents of a tea bag.

equipment and techniques

equipment

KNIVES

Knives are an essential tool in the kitchen. Low-quality knives dull quickly, and are not only fatiguing to work with but also hazardous. Select knives with comfortable handles that fit your hand. Although I have a fine Chinese cleaver, I prefer my 8-inch chef's knife that is just the right weight and size for my hands.

RICE COOKERS

A rice cooker can save you a lot of time. It can cook rice and rice porridges to perfection, as well as steam foods without close supervision. There are many varieties of rice cookers on the market. Decide on an appropriate size for your family, and then select the features you would like to have.

A basic rice cooker simply cooks the rice and then shuts off. High-end rice cookers offer many other features, like induction heating for energy efficiency or "neuro-fuzzy logic" to make fine adjustments as the rice cooks to achieve better results, and keep the rice moist and warm for up to 12 hours. I can program my Zojirushi "neuro-fuzzy logic" rice cooker in the morning so it begins to cook rice in time for the evening's meal. It offers different settings for cooking white or brown rice, or porridges.

SKILLETS AND SAUTÉ PANS

A skillet or frying pan has sloping sides. It is ideal for flipping and tossing food, and good for pan-frying and making omelets. You may need to purchase a lid separately. I have a chef's pan with deep sloping sides, which serves most of my everyday cooking needs.

A sauté pan has higher, vertical sides. It can be used for cooking dishes with lots of liquid.

Skillets and sauté pans range from 7 to 14 inches in diameter. If you want only one, buy a 10- or 12-inch pan, and preferably one with a lid, which is suitable for a family of four.

If you are using nonstick, look for a skillet made without PFCs. These pans are marketed as "green" or "eco-friendly" and have a ceramic-based surface coating that won't break down when used over high heat.

STEAMERS

There are many types of steamers on the market, including steamer inserts for standard cookware, bamboo steamers, and electric countertop steamers.

When steaming food, be sure to lift the lid up and away from you to protect yourself from scalding steam. Check the water level often and add more water as necessary. Be sure the food is placed above the water level to avoid submerging the food.

Even if you don't own a steamer, you can still use other kitchen equipment to steam food. To use a wok as a steamer, and prevent the steam racks from scratching the bottom of a nonstick wok or pan, set the rack on a heatproof plate. If you don't have a rack, use a small, heatproof bowl, filled with water, and place the plate of food on top. Fill your wok about one-third full with hot water and bring to a boil. Cover and steam as instructed in the recipe.

WOKS

A wok is a versatile utensil for stir-frying, steaming (see above), and even cooking soup. In the homes of many families in Asia, the wok is the main cooking utensil. Choose a high-quality, cast-iron or carbon-steel wok. The nonstick coating on inexpensive woks can peel off over time. A good choice for everyday use is either a 12-inch or 14-inch size.

I prefer a flat-bottomed wok to a round-bottomed one because it sits directly on the burner, working effectively on both electric and gas ranges. Purchase a snug-fitting lid if your wok doesn't have one; it's handy for steaming and prevents spattering. Wok lids made of aluminum are the lightest and most inexpensive.

If you don't have a wok, don't let that stop you. A high, slope-sided skillet or chef's pan works just as well.

techniques

CUTTING

Today, you can buy precut fresh or frozen vegetables or use an electric food processor to do the slicing and chopping for you. However, I still enjoy the traditional method of cutting vegetables with a knife. A good set of knives is imperative. While cutting ingredients can be time-consuming, it can also be relaxing. I enjoy playing classical music while cutting ingredients, making the task a meditative experience.

When cutting ingredients for Asian-style cooking, the goal is to create uniform, bite-size pieces so that all of the ingredients will cook evenly and create an attractive presentation.

Seasonings and garnishes such as fresh herbs should be minced, so their flavors can be easily absorbed into the dish.

slicing. Hold the food firmly on the cutting board with one hand while holding the knife securely in your dominant hand. Cut straight down to produce even slices.

julienne and shredding. Stack a few slices and cut straight down, using an even slicing technique to create sticks. To shred into slivers, cut the food into paper-thin slices before cutting across the same way to create thin strips. For matchsticks or julienne, start with ⅛-inch slices. Cut these slices into ⅛-inch sticks.

dicing. Line sticks up perpendicular to the blade. Cut straight down, creating ¼-inch cubes.

mincing. Cut the ingredient into thin strips and dice the strips. Control the knife with a firm grip on the handle, with the other hand holding down the blunt end of the tip against the board. Using the tip as a pivot, rock the knife up and down in a rapid chopping motion, moving it from side to side to mince the food evenly. Occasionally regroup the food, using the dull side of the knife to gather the ingredient. Repeat the process until the food is cut into the desired, even size.

roll cutting. When preparing long vegetables like cucumbers and carrots, roll cutting makes aesthetically pleasing chunks and exposes more surface area. Holding the blade perpendicular to the board, cut down along the diagonal. Roll the vegetable a quarter-turn before repeating the same cut at the same angle. Continue to roll and cut along the length of the vegetable.

MARINATING

Marinating is one of the cornerstones of Asian cuisine. It serves a variety of purposes: tenderizing, sealing in flavors, and moderating strong smell in seafood and meat. Marinating times vary by recipe and cooking methods.

Marinating raw meat, fish, tofu, and vegetables with sauces or dry spices can take anywhere from 15 minutes to overnight. I like to avoid using plastic containers if I'm marinating foods for a long time, as plastic and aluminum can alter the taste. Use nonreactive containers like glass, stainless steel, or ceramic and always refrigerate marinated foods. To use a marinade for raw meat or seafood as a sauce, it must be heated to a full boil in order to be safe to consume. Otherwise, discard it.

MIXING SAUCES

Pairing sauces with the right dishes is similar to pairing wine with a meal. Most sauces are versatile and can be used for marinating, dipping, or stir-frying. They liven up dishes and can often serve as a key ingredient. Prepare the sauce before you start cooking to give the flavors time to blend. Make extra so you will have them at hand when needed. Most of the sauces in this book can last up to 5 days in a sealed container in the refrigerator.

SIMMERING

A slow cooking process, often used to cook stews, soups, and sauces, simmering allows foods to absorb more flavors. To achieve a simmer, bring the liquid to a full boil, then reduce the heat to just below the boiling point.

STEAMING

In Asia, steaming is second in popularity only to stir-frying as a cooking technique, in part because most kitchens are not equipped with ovens. Seafood, meat, vegetables, custards, filled buns, dumplings, and even desserts are frequently steamed.

Steaming works by suspending food over boiling water. The hot vapors given off from the water surround and cook the food, allowing ingredients to retain their vitamins, minerals, moisture, and flavors. It gives food a clean, delicate taste and is an ideal technique for those who want to enjoy light, healthful meals.

The traditional way to steam is to place food in a stack of bamboo steamers over a wok or large pot with water. A dish with sloping sides will prevent the food from spilling over, and make it easier to remove after the cooking is completed. You can also steam food without the bamboo steamers. See the section on Steamers (page 19). Below are a few helpful steps:

- When using a dish to hold the food, always make sure it is heat-resistant; it should also be slightly smaller than the steamer.

- Bring the water to a boil before placing the food to be steamed in the steamer.

- Once the food is in the steamer, cover it so that the food heats evenly and efficiently.

- Dumplings can go directly on a rack or a steamer basket lined with thinly sliced carrots or cabbage leaves to prevent the food from sticking, thus eliminating the need to oil the steamer.

- Steaming requires lots of water. Check the water level as the food cooks, and replenish the water as necessary. Keep a teapot full of hot water next to the steamer.

- Don't submerge the food or you'll end up boiling it. Keep it above the water level at all times.

- Don't crowd the food. Make sure there is enough space between items so the steam can circulate evenly.

- Wear oven mitts when putting in and removing food from a steamer. There are excellent silicone mitts available. Always lift the lid up and away from you, so your hands, arms, and face are not exposed to scalding steam.

STIR-FRYING

Stir-frying is the most common Asian cooking technique. This method begins by heating up oil and stir-frying dry or fresh spices such as ginger, garlic, chiles, green tea, or sesame seeds to flavor the oil. Other ingredients, sauces, and seasonings are then added in their proper order during the cooking. The food is stirred constantly.

Stir-fried dishes take just minutes to prepare. Stir-frying is an ideal cooking method for a busy, modern lifestyle and a perfect way to prepare tasty, healthy meals, because it requires very little oil, the cooking time is short, and the food retains its natural flavors, nutrients, and textures.

Traditional stir-frying requires a lot of chopping, complex seasonings, and a wok. When time is of the essence, use precut vegetables and sliced meats that are readily available in supermarkets, along with store-bought sauces and flavored oils.

Ready: Stir-frying is like getting on a roller coaster—once you start, there's no stopping. Make sure you have all your ingredients cut, meats marinated, and sauces mixed. Arrange everything near the wok, including the serving plate and garnishes. To ensure even and fast cooking, most of the recipes in this book call for thinly sliced or shredded ingredients (see page 20). Set the table. That's right! Stir-fried food tastes its best when it is hot. You don't want your hot creation getting cold and soggy.

Set: Stir-frying is usually done in batches of ingredients, and the order in which the ingredients are added is important. Aromatic seasonings like green tea, ginger, and garlic usually go in first, followed by meats or seafood, and firm vegetables such as carrots go in before softer ones such as spinach. Add the sauce when the other ingredients are partially cooked.

Go: Preheat the skillet or wok for a minute before adding the oil. Swirl it to coat the surface and heat the oil. If the recipe calls for dry green tea leaves, garlic, ginger, or chile pepper, this is the time to add it. With practice you can judge by the cooking sounds and smells. The purpose here is to flavor the oil and release the fragrance of the seasonings. Quickly add the other ingredients and cover immediately to prevent splattering. Keep the food moving by giving the wok a couple of good shakes. After a few seconds of shaking, and when the moisture from the food has cooked off, you can safely remove the lid and start stir-frying.

Use your spatula to toss the food over the surface of the wok or pan, so that everything cooks evenly. I prefer to use a heat-resistant silicone spatula, which can handle temperatures up to 650°F (345°C).

Don't forget to taste the dish before you transfer it to the serving plate. Many recipes call for seasoning with salt and pepper to taste. This is the time to taste and adjust the seasoning. If adding sesame oil, put it in at the last minute, since its flavor tends to evaporate when exposed to high heat.

sauces and con- diments

In some rural Asian communities, matchmakers still busily shuttle among the families and homes of eligible young men and women to arrange marriages.

When my grandmother made sauces she would say, "Let's do some matchmaking today." She had many fresh ingredients set around the table with empty ceramic jars nearby. Like a magician, she threw together a little of this and that, and soon a variety of sauces emerged. Grandma told me, "The key is to match flavors that will complement each other," by balancing the yin (cooling) ingredients with yang (warming).

Grandmother never made the same sauce twice, yet they were always delicious. For years I "match-made" sauces Grandmother's way, until I wrote some down, which resulted in the recipes that follow.

Before you begin, have plenty of small containers with lids available for storing different sauces. You can reuse condiment jars or buy containers from supermarkets or at cookware stores. Most sauces can be made ahead and stored in a tightly sealed container in the refrigerator. To keep it fresh, always use a clean, dry spoon when you use the sauce.

You should use the following recipes as a starting point, and let your own idea of a good marriage be your guide. If the chile is too hot for your taste, use less or omit it entirely. With practice, you, too, will become an experienced matchmaker.

chile-garlic sauce

Serving dumplings and spring rolls without a dipping sauce would be like painting a dragon without dotting the eyes. Ever since he was three years old, my son always knew to set the dipping bowls out when I started making dumplings. This sauce is one of his favorites. It pairs well with Green Tea–Steamed Shrimp Dumplings (page 195) or Crisp Apple-Chicken Spring Rolls (page 110).

MAKES ABOUT ¾ CUP SAUCE

¼ cup reduced-sodium soy sauce

¼ cup brewed green tea (see page 15)

2 tablespoons fresh lemon juice

2 tablespoons rice vinegar

2 teaspoons toasted sesame oil

2 teaspoons honey

1 fresh red chile pepper, seeded and minced

2 garlic cloves, minced

1 green onion, minced

1. Combine all of the ingredients in a bowl. Cover and refrigerate for 30 minutes or longer to allow the flavors to meld.

2. Use immediately, or store in the refrigerator in a tightly sealed glass container for up to 5 days.

sun-dried tomato–green tea sauce

When I first saw sun-dried tomatoes, they reminded me of how I used to watch my grandmother dry vegetables in the summer. We would sit together under a shady tree stringing up daikon, carrots, and cabbage while she told me captivating folktales.

In Asia, bell peppers are a common seasoning, while sun-dried tomatoes are considered exotic. After tasting a sun-dried tomato sauce at an Italian restaurant, I was inspired to combine it with roasted red peppers. Accented by green tea and rice vinegar, the result was this unique East-Meets-West sauce.

You can use the sauce for garnishing noodle dishes, or as a condiment. Some of my friends even use it as a spread for their turkey and roast beef sandwiches.

MAKES ABOUT 1½ CUPS SAUCE

1 cup fresh or jarred roasted red bell peppers, drained

2 tablespoons (about 1 ounce) dry-packed sun-dried tomatoes, chopped

2 garlic cloves, peeled

½ cup brewed green tea (see page 15)

2 tablespoons rice vinegar

1 tablespoon extra-virgin olive oil

½ teaspoon ground white pepper

1. Combine all of the ingredients in a blender or food processor and process until smooth. Refrigerate in a tightly sealed glass container for 30 minutes or longer to allow the flavors to meld.

2. Use immediately, or store in the refrigerator for up to 5 days.

ginger tea sauce

I like to make this versatile sauce at least a day in advance to allow the flavors to marry. You can use it to marinate turkey, chicken, tofu, and fish. Double or triple the recipe if you are marinating a large turkey.

MAKES ABOUT 1 CUP SAUCE

¼ cup extra-virgin olive oil

¼ cup brewed white or green tea (see page 15)

2 tablespoons fresh lemon juice

2 tablespoons soy sauce

6 garlic cloves, minced

3 tablespoons minced fresh chives

1 teaspoon minced fresh serrano or other chile pepper (optional)

1 tablespoon minced fresh ginger

1. Place all of the ingredients in a bowl. Cover and refrigerate for 30 minutes or longer to allow the flavors to meld.

2. Use immediately, or store in the refrigerator in a tightly sealed glass container for up to 3 days.

green tea–orange sauce

As a little girl, one of my chores was to set out the orange peels in the sunlight and collect them once dried. My grandmother would then store them in a ceramic jar and use them throughout the cold months. Now, I feel so fortunate that I can buy fresh oranges year-round so I don't have to go through the trouble of drying orange peels.

Orange peels frequently appear in stir-fries, soups, and sauces. They aid digestion and clear mucus from the throat and lungs. This mild sauce, flavored with orange and green tea, goes well with dumplings or grilled dishes such as Green Tea–Steamed Shrimp Dumplings (page 195), Scallop, Onion, and Pepper Kebabs (page 180), and Sea Bass with Grilled Bananas (page 182).

MAKES ABOUT 1 CUP SAUCE

¼ cup extra-virgin olive oil

1 tablespoon grated orange zest

2 teaspoons loose green tea leaves

⅓ cup soy sauce

3 tablespoons rice vinegar

4 green onions, white parts only, minced

1. Heat the oil in a small saucepan over medium heat. Add the orange zest and tea and sauté until fragrant. Remove from the heat.

2. Add the soy sauce and vinegar. Stir in the green onions. Refrigerate in a tightly sealed glass container for 30 minutes or longer to allow the flavors to meld.

3. Use immediately, or store in the refrigerator for up to 5 days.

sweet-and-sour chile sauce

When my son was little he loved to help me make this sauce after school. He would run around with his lemongrass sword, fighting imaginary aliens, and then help me gather ingredients. There are many varieties of bottled sweet and sour chile sauces on the market. However, none of them can compare in taste to a fresh, homemade sauce that's low in sodium and free of MSG. This sauce will enhance any meat or seafood dishes.

MAKES ABOUT ½ CUP SAUCE

1 lemongrass stalk

1 fresh red chile pepper, seeded and minced

2 teaspoons brown sugar

3 tablespoons fish sauce

¼ cup fresh lime juice

1. Remove the tough outer layers and green parts of the lemongrass. Mince the tender portion of the stalk.

2. Combine the lemongrass, chile, sugar, fish sauce, and lime juice in a bowl. Cover and refrigerate for 30 minutes or longer to allow the flavors to meld.

3. Use immediately, or store in the refrigerator in a tightly sealed glass container for up to 5 days.

lime-soy-ginger sauce

This simple sauce goes well with spring rolls as a dipping sauce. Also, it makes a good marinade for seafood. I once served grilled trout marinated in this sauce to a friend who disliked fish—it completely changed his mind!

MAKES ABOUT ½ CUP SAUCE

¼ cup low-sodium soy sauce

1 tablespoon rice vinegar

2 tablespoons fresh lime juice

1½ teaspoons sesame oil

1 tablespoon thinly shredded fresh ginger

1 green onion, green part only, minced

2 teaspoons black sesame seeds, toasted (see Note)

1. Combine all of the ingredients in a bowl. Cover and refrigerate for 30 minutes or longer to allow the flavors to meld.

2. Use immediately, or store in the refrigerator in a tightly sealed glass container for up to 5 days.

NOTE: Sesame seeds can be purchased already toasted, but to toast your own, preheat the oven to 350°F (177°C). Spread the sesame seeds out on a baking sheet in a single layer. Bake for 5 to 6 minutes, or until the sesame seeds are crisp and fragrant. Watch them carefully so they don't burn.

miso-sesame sauce

Although miso originated in Asia, it is now widely used throughout the international culinary landscape. After I learned the health benefits of turmeric and ginger, I decided to "match-make" them with miso, a good source of antioxidants and two important minerals, manganese and zinc. In my interpretation of this traditional sauce, I like to use fresh turmeric when available. However, fresh ginger is a delicious alternative. This sauce makes a wonderful complement to Turmeric Scallops with Turnips and Cashews (page 144) or Steamed Asparagus (page 191).

MAKES ABOUT ¾ CUP SAUCE

3 tablespoons white miso

4½ teaspoons black sesame seeds, toasted (see page 32)

2 tablespoons rice vinegar

1½ teaspoons fresh turmeric or ginger, minced

¼ cup soy milk

1 tablespoon sesame oil

1. Mix the miso, sesame seeds, rice vinegar, and turmeric in a bowl. Slowly add the soy milk, whisking well. Stir in the sesame oil. Add more liquid, if desired, for a thinner sauce. Cover and refrigerate for 30 minutes or longer to allow the flavors to meld.

2. Use immediately, or store in the refrigerator in a tightly sealed glass container for up to 5 days.

curry-peanut sauce

Use this versatile condiment as a marinade for chicken, pork, or beef. I often make a large batch and also use it on whole wheat noodles and steamed or grilled dishes, such as Tofu Filled with Crabmeat and Pork (page 193) or Beef and Vegetable Kebabs (page 168). For a smooth texture, process this sauce in a food processor for 20 seconds before cooling.

MAKES ABOUT 1½ CUPS SAUCE

1 tablespoon extra-virgin olive oil

2 garlic cloves, minced

1 teaspoon grated fresh ginger

¼ cup minced onion

½ cup unsalted peanut butter

½ cup rice milk or soy milk

1½ teaspoons fresh lemon juice

1 teaspoon curry powder

1. In a small saucepan, heat the oil over medium heat. Add the garlic, ginger, and onion and sauté until the onion softens, 4 to 5 minutes.

2. Add the peanut butter, rice milk, lemon juice, and curry powder. Cook, stirring, until the sauce is hot and the peanut butter melts, 1 to 2 minutes. Let the sauce cool.

3. Use immediately, or store in the refrigerator in a tightly sealed glass container for up to 1 week.

lime-peanut sauce

This is another version of my favorite peanut sauce. It works well with noodle dishes, such as Pad Thai with Tofu and Pine Nuts (page 151), or as a dip for steamed vegetables or grilled seafood. For a vegetarian version, substitute vegetable stock or soy milk for the chicken stock.

MAKES ABOUT 1 CUP SAUCE

1 tablespoon olive oil

1 garlic clove, minced

1 fresh chile, such as jalapeño or serrano, seeded and minced

1 teaspoon minced fresh ginger

½ cup low-sodium chicken stock or vegetable stock

3 tablespoons fresh lime juice

¼ cup unsalted creamy peanut butter

2 tablespoons brown sugar

Fish sauce

1. In a small saucepan, heat the oil over medium heat. Add the garlic, chile, and ginger and sauté until softened, 4 to 5 minutes. Reduce the heat to low.

2. Add the chicken stock, lime juice, peanut butter, and sugar. Cook, stirring, until the peanut butter melts, 1 to 2 minutes. Add fish sauce to taste.

3. Use immediately, or store in the refrigerator in a tightly sealed glass container for up to 1 week.

spicy honey-basil sauce

In the summertime when I go to the farmers' market, the smell of fresh basil always compels me to put it in my basket. Basil promotes yin and lowers blood sugar levels. It also aids with digestion. Use this sauce as a dipping sauce or salad dressing.

MAKES ABOUT 1 CUP SAUCE

2 American ginseng tea bags

1 cup boiling spring water

½ cup packed fresh basil leaves

2 garlic cloves, minced

1 small fresh or dried red chile pepper or 1 medium jalapeño chile, chopped (include the seeds if you like it spicy)

2 tablespoons pine nuts, toasted (see page 99)

2 tablespoons fresh lemon juice

2 tablespoons olive oil

1 tablespoon honey

¼ teaspoon salt

¼ teaspoon ground white pepper

1. Brew the tea bags in the boiling spring water for 5 minutes. Place the contents of the tea bags and the tea in a blender, and discard the bags.

2. Add the remaining ingredients to the blender and process until puréed. Refrigerate in a tightly sealed glass container for 30 minutes or longer to allow the flavors to meld.

3. Use immediately, or store in the refrigerator for up to 3 days.

spicy sesame sauce

Toasted sesame has a boisterous flavor that balances well with green onions, soy sauce, and lemon juice. Aside from making a wonderful dipping sauce, this also makes an unusual and delicious salad dressing. I often double the recipe for this versatile sauce and store the extra in a tightly sealed container in the refrigerator. It always speeds up my cooking on a busy night.

MAKES ABOUT ¾ CUP SAUCE

2 garlic cloves, minced

1 green onion, green and white parts, finely sliced

1 teaspoon minced fresh ginger

1 teaspoon thinly shredded fresh red chile pepper

1 teaspoon white sesame seeds, toasted (see page 32)

¼ cup soy sauce

2 tablespoons fresh lemon juice

1 teaspoon sesame oil

1. Place all of the ingredients in a bowl and mix to combine. Cover and store in the refrigerator for 30 minutes or longer to allow the flavors to meld.

2. Use immediately, or store in a tightly sealed glass container in the refrigerator for up to 3 days.

papaya-mango salsa

Be sure to use ripe papayas and mangoes. They should be fragrant and slightly soft when pressed with your thumb. Serve this salsa with grilled tofu, seafood, or poultry, or as a dip for chips, crackers, and toasted bread. This condiment is my guests' favorite when I host a summer party.

MAKES ABOUT 3 CUPS SALSA

1 mango, peeled, pitted, and cut into ¼-inch cubes

1 small papaya, peeled, seeded, and cut into ¼-inch cubes

1 small fresh red chile pepper, seeded and diced

1 small red onion, minced (about ¾ cup)

¼ cup chopped fresh cilantro leaves

1 tablespoon fresh lemon juice

1 tablespoon white wine vinegar

Salt

Freshly ground black pepper

1. In a medium bowl, mix the mango, papaya, chile, onion, cilantro, lemon juice, and vinegar. Season to taste with salt and pepper.

2. Cover and chill in the refrigerator for 30 minutes or longer to allow the flavors to meld. The salsa can be stored in the refrigerator for up to 3 days.

mango-ginger salsa

Fresh mango, combined with ginger and lemon juice, gives this salsa a wonderfully refreshing flavor. This vibrant salsa is easy to make and perfect with grilled salmon, vegetables, and tofu. It also makes a great dip for chips and crackers. Once you taste this salsa, you may be reluctant to use a store-bought version again!

MAKES ABOUT 2½ CUPS SALSA

1 large ripe mango, peeled, pitted, and cut into ¼-inch cubes

1 small red onion, minced (about ¾ cup)

½ cup chopped watercress

2 teaspoons minced fresh ginger

2 tablespoons fresh lemon juice

2 teaspoons extra-virgin olive oil

Salt

1. In a medium bowl, mix together the mango, onion, watercress, ginger, and lemon juice. Season to taste with salt.

2. Cover and chill in the refrigerator for 30 minutes or longer to allow the flavors to meld. The salsa can be stored in the refrigerator for up to 3 days.

essential thai peanut sauce

This sauce was inspired by one of my visits to Thailand. I modernized it by using almond butter and soy milk and adding more fresh seasonings. Once you have tried this all-purpose, versatile sauce, you will find many creative ways to use it to liven up nontraditional dishes. I have served it as a dip for organic blue corn chips and as a topping for baguette slices. It is especially delicious with grilled tofu, vegetables, and seafood. For a smoother texture, purée it in a blender.

MAKES ABOUT 1 CUP SAUCE

2 tablespoons almond butter or peanut butter

½ cup plain soy milk

¼ cup low-fat unsweetened coconut milk

2 tablespoons fresh lime juice

1 tablespoon fish sauce, or more to taste

1 tablespoon honey

4 garlic cloves, minced

1 medium fresh red chile pepper, such as Fresno, seeded and minced

1 green onion, minced

1 tablespoon chopped fresh cilantro leaves

1. Place the almond or peanut butter in a medium bowl. Slowly whisk in the soy milk, coconut milk, lime juice, fish sauce to taste, and honey to make a smooth paste. Stir in the garlic, chile, green onion, and cilantro.

2. Use immediately, or store in the refrigerator in a tightly sealed glass container for up to 1 week.

savory green tea oil

The fragrant flavor of green tea adds inspiration to this oil. You can use it for stir-fries, or drizzle a few teaspoons over a finished dish before serving. For that extra spicy kick, I keep the seeds in the chiles when mincing them.

MAKES ABOUT ½ CUP OIL

1 teaspoon plus ¼ cup extra-virgin olive oil

2 teaspoons loose green tea

5 garlic cloves, minced

1 tablespoon minced fresh ginger

2 fresh red chile peppers, minced

2 green onions, white parts only, minced

½ teaspoon salt

1. In a small saucepan, heat the 1 teaspoon of oil. Add the green tea and cook, stirring, until the tea is fragrant and crispy, about 1 minute.

2. Place the tea, garlic, ginger, chiles, green onions, and salt in a short wide-mouth canning jar and mix to combine.

3. In the same saucepan, heat the remaining ¼ cup oil until it is very hot. Carefully pour the hot oil over the contents of the jar. Partially cover the jar and set aside to cool. Seal the jar tightly and store in the refrigerator for up to 2 weeks. Stir the sauce before using.

NOTE: Wear rubber gloves when mincing chiles. Turn the kitchen fan on before pouring the oil over the chile mixture.

cucumber raita

After tasting raita at an Indian restaurant, I decided to develop my own version. This cooling and refreshing condiment works nicely to balance any spicy dishes or grilled meat.

MAKES ABOUT 1½ CUPS RAITA

1 cup low-fat plain yogurt

1 tablespoon fresh lime juice

1 small cucumber, peeled, seeded, and diced

1 small garlic clove, minced

2 tablespoons chopped fresh mint leaves

½ teaspoon ground cumin

¼ teaspoon salt

¼ teaspoon freshly ground black pepper

COMBINE all of the ingredients in a small bowl. Serve immediately, or cover and refrigerate for 30 minutes to allow the flavors to meld. Stored covered, the raita will keep in the refrigerator for up to 3 days.

mediterranean dip

This zesty dip was inspired by my visit to the Mediterranean. It can be served on toasted whole wheat bread or crackers, with raw or blanched vegetables, or try it with sliced tofu that has been baked for 10 minutes in a 350°F (177°C) oven. Japanese eggplants are smaller and more delicate than common eggplants and are often a lighter shade.

MAKES 8 SERVINGS

3 medium red or yellow tomatoes

2 small zucchini

2 Japanese eggplants

2 small yellow squash

¼ cup onion, minced

1 tablespoon minced fresh turmeric or 1 tablespoon dried turmeric powder

1 teaspoon ground cumin

1 tablespoon extra-virgin olive oil

3 tablespoons fresh orange juice

Salt

1. Preheat an outdoor grill or broiler. Halve the tomatoes, zucchini, eggplants, and squash lengthwise. Grill or broil the vegetables until softened and lightly browned on both sides. Set aside to cool.

2. When cool enough to handle, chop the vegetables into small pieces and toss them together in a large bowl. Mix in the onion, turmeric, cumin, oil, orange juice, and salt to taste. Cover and chill in the refrigerator for about 30 minutes.

3. Use immediately, or store in a covered container in the refrigerator for up to 3 days.

match-making in a pot

stocks, soups, stews, and hot pots

In my hometown of Wuhan in central China, winter is an endless succession of chilly, gray, and damp days. When I was growing up during the Cultural Revolution, food was rationed.

I always looked forward to mealtimes. Grandmother's stew was one of my favorites. I watched her intensely as she sliced meat, boiled fish cakes, and cut up tofu. It always took hours to cook a stew on our small coal-burning stove. As the cooking warmed our small apartment, my brothers and I would huddle around and feast on the delicious smell.

Asian cultures consider stock-based dishes such as soups, stews, and hot pots to be one of the best ways to reap the health benefits of foods, as the slow process of simmering ingredients allows their flavors to meld. They can be served with other dishes or alone as simple one-dish meals.

In cold weather, Grandmother would serve us warming stews that boost yang energies to strengthen the immune system. On warm days, Grandmother would serve us light, cooling soups, which were also intended as a beverage to quench thirst. Even after living in the United States for over twenty-five years, I am still baffled to see people drink ice water with their meals in restaurants on cold days, completely contrary to the TCM principles of yin and yang.

One summer, when I brought a group of my American students to China, they were puzzled that instead of ice water, the waitress brought them soup. They were fascinated when I explained to them that the Chinese drink cooling soup in hot weather because it promotes the production of bodily fluids, moisturizes the skin, and relieves dry coughs.

The following recipes offer a varied selection of satisfying stews and soups for different seasons. Take the time to cook and enjoy these savory dishes. They will compel you to take a break from your busy lifestyle and appreciate the beauty of food.

tips on making soup

plan ahead. For fast and delicious cooking, good stocks are a must. Make them in advance and keep them in your freezer or refrigerator. Refrigerated, stock will keep for 3 or 4 days. Frozen, it will keep for up to 1 month. If you are cooking for one or two people, you can halve the ingredients.

use fresh ingredients. Well made, nourishing soups and stews start with stocks made with fresh ingredients. While homemade stock is preferable, organic store-bought stock, soy milk, rice milk, coconut milk, or water can be substituted in some instances.

multitask. Good stocks take time to cook, but they do not demand your constant attention. When I was young, my grandmother often started her day by combining fresh ingredients and water in a big pot and bringing them to a boil. When she lowered the stock to a simmer, I knew that it was time for me to fetch my comb, as she would be free to braid my hair and get me ready for school.

tailor to your liking. For a thick stock, place everything in a blender and blend until smooth. For a lighter stock, strain the ingredients and pour the stock into a container that can be tightly sealed. Enjoy the strained ingredients, such as chicken and vegetables, with rice or noodles.

mix and match. Recipes throughout this book call for different stocks. If you don't have one on hand and are pressed for time, don't let it stop you. Mix and match your own or use purchased stocks as a base and enhance them with your favorite fresh ingredients.

healthy homemade chicken stock

Many chicken stock recipes call for chicken bones or a whole chicken. This healthy, simpler version uses aseptically packaged organic chicken broth as the base, which shortens the cooking time and cuts down the fat. The corn gives the stock a slightly sweet flavor and the Asian ginseng adds to the yang balance. Use it as a soup base or pour it over cooked noodles and vegetables. The warming ginger, garlic, and onion in the stock will help you combat the damp and chill of cold weather.

MAKES ABOUT 5½ CUPS STOCK

2 tablespoons extra-virgin olive oil

2 tablespoons diced fresh ginger

6 garlic cloves, minced

1 medium onion, chopped

1 pound boneless, skinless chicken breasts, cut into 1-inch pieces

3 cups water

6 cups store-bought organic chicken stock

2 to 3 whole fresh ginseng roots (about 1 ounce) (optional)

3 cups fresh or frozen sweet corn kernels

Salt

Ground white pepper

1. Heat a wok or nonstick skillet over medium heat and coat it with the oil. Add the ginger, garlic, and onion and sauté until fragrant, 1 to 2 minutes. Add the chicken and sauté until lightly browned, 2 to 3 minutes.

2. In a large pot, bring the water and the chicken broth to a boil. Add the chicken mixture, ginseng, and corn kernels and bring to a boil. Reduce the heat and simmer for 50 to 60 minutes. Season to taste with salt and pepper.

3. Strain the liquid through a colander, pressing out as much liquid as possible. Set aside to cool. Transfer the stock to an airtight container and refrigerate for up to 3 days, or freeze for up to 1 month.

fresh vegetable stock

Although a variety of vegetable stocks are available in supermarkets, nothing tastes like homemade stock. Use only the freshest vegetables in season. They blend together to form a rich base for many soups and sauces. For a spicy version, add two fresh chiles.

MAKES ABOUT 5 CUPS STOCK

3 tablespoons extra-virgin olive oil

1 tablespoon chopped fresh ginger

3 garlic cloves, minced

1½ cups fresh shiitake or oyster mushrooms, cut into small pieces

1 cup chopped leeks, white parts only

1 cup snow peas

6 cups water

3 medium tomatoes, chopped

3 cups fresh or frozen corn kernels

2 teaspoons sesame oil

Salt

Freshly ground black pepper

1. Heat a wok or nonstick skillet over medium heat and coat it with the oil. Add the ginger, garlic, mushrooms, and leeks and sauté until the mushrooms are lightly browned, about 1 minute. Add the snow peas and sauté until softened, about 2 minutes.

2. Add the water, tomatoes, and corn kernels and bring to a boil. Reduce the heat and simmer for 45 minutes. Stir in the sesame oil. Season to taste with salt and pepper.

3. Strain the liquid through a colander, pressing out as much liquid as possible. Set aside to cool. Transfer the stock to an airtight container and refrigerate for up to 3 days, or freeze for up to 1 month.

exotic green tea fish stock

Many recipes for seafood stock call for fish heads and bones, which can be hard to find, so I use scallops and chunks of firm, white fish. After the stock is prepared, enjoy the seafood over rice or noodles. This stock makes for a tasty base for the Pumpkin-Seafood Pot (page 77) and the Tomato and Crabmeat Egg Drop Soup (page 67).

MAKES ABOUT 4½ CUPS STOCK

6 green tea bags

8 cups boiling water

2 tablespoons extra-virgin olive oil

2 tablespoons diced fresh ginger

4 garlic cloves, quartered

1 cup minced fresh oyster or shiitake mushrooms

1 fresh red chile pepper, minced

2 medium leeks, white parts only, cut diagonally into ½-inch pieces

½ pound bay scallops

½ pound white fish fillet, such as sole, sea bass, or catfish, cut into 2-inch pieces

12 sprigs fresh cilantro

1 teaspoon ground white pepper

1. Place the green tea bags in a large pot. Add the boiling water and simmer over low heat for 3 minutes. Using a slotted spoon, scoop up the tea bags. With the back of a separate spoon, press the tea out of the tea bags, then discard the bags.

2. Heat a wok or nonstick skillet over medium heat and coat it with the oil. Add the ginger, garlic, mushrooms, chile, and leeks and sauté until the leeks soften and become fragrant, about 2 minutes.

3. Transfer the vegetable mixture to the pot with the tea and bring the mixture to a boil. Add the scallops, fish, and cilantro and return to a boil. Reduce the heat and simmer, uncovered, for 40 minutes. Season with the white pepper.

4. Strain the liquid through a colander, pressing out as much liquid as possible. Set aside to cool. Transfer the stock to an airtight container and refrigerate for up to 3 days, or freeze for up to 1 month.

cold papaya soup

Years ago, I was assigned to develop a six-course meal using papaya for a featured food article. For weeks, I served my family papaya dishes at every meal. Even today, my son jokes that he was traumatized by the experience, though some of his favorite summer dishes originated from that assignment. This cooling, refreshing soup makes a wonderful beginning to a summer meal.

MAKES 6 SERVINGS

½ large ripe papaya, peeled and chopped (about 1 cups), seeds reserved and refrigerated

1 small cucumber, peeled, seeded, and chopped

¾ cup fruit or vanilla soy yogurt

½ cup soy creamer

1 tablespoon honey

1 tablespoon fresh lime juice

Fresh mint leaves, minced, for garnish

1. Place the papaya, cucumber, yogurt, soy creamer, honey, and lime juice in a blender. Purée until smooth.

2. Cover and store in the refrigerator for 30 minutes. Divide the soup equally among six fruit cups or soup bowls. Place a dab of the reserved papaya seeds in the center, and garnish with the mint around the seeds.

chilled cucumber soup with rose petals

This soothing, cooling soup is loaded with ingredients such as cooling cucumbers, soy yogurt, and mint. It will nourish your skin and maintain its moisture during summer. Serve it on hot days to counteract the irritating effects of excessive heat and humidity. I use organic roses from my garden. If you don't grow your own, make sure the rose petals used for cooking are pesticide-free.

MAKES 4 SERVINGS

2 cups plain soy yogurt

3 Japanese or 1 English cucumber, peeled, seeded, and chopped

¼ cup chopped fresh mint leaves

2 tablespoons fresh lemon juice

2 teaspoons ground cumin

Salt

Small petals from the center of an organically grown, pesticide-free rose, for garnish

Fresh mint leaves, for garnish

PLACE the yogurt, cucumber, mint, lemon juice, and cumin in a blender and purée until smooth. Season with salt to taste. Divide equally among four bowls. Garnish with the rose petals and mint leaves.

the empress's secret beauty soup

Legend has it that a version of this soup was a favorite of a Chinese empress and the concubines in the Forbidden City. In China, watermelon rind is thought to have a cooling effect. During the summer months, my grand-mother used it in salads, soups, and stir-fries. The yin-neutral combination of green tea and barley is believed to keep skin smooth, firm, and elastic.

If you don't have kasha, you can add more oats or substitute another grain like rye. Serve this soup for lunch or as an elegant first course for dinner.

MAKES 4 SERVINGS

¼ cup rolled oats

¼ cup wheat berries

¼ cup barley

¼ cup brown rice

¼ cup kasha (buckwheat groats)

3 cups watermelon rind, cut into 4-inch-wide strips

6 cups plus 1½ cups water

½ cup rock sugar, broken into small pieces

2 green tea bags

1. In a large saucepan, combine the oats, wheat berries, barley, rice, kasha, watermelon rind, and the 6 cups of water and bring to a boil. Cover, reduce the heat to low, and simmer until the liquid has reduced to 4 cups, about 50 minutes.

2. In a small saucepan, combine the rock sugar, tea bags, and the remaining 1½ cups water and bring to a boil. Reduce the heat to medium-low, simmer for 2 minutes, and then remove and discard the tea bags. Continue to simmer the mixture until the rock sugar has dissolved.

3. Remove and discard the watermelon rind. Divide the soup equally among four bowls and flavor with the sugar and green tea mixture to taste. Serve warm or at room temperature.

nourishing ribs with goji berries and red dates

To this day, I remember how when my son was little, he struggled to spear a slice of daikon from the soup with his chopsticks. When he succeeded, he would give it a quick dip in the sauce and slurp it down happily.

TCM doctors believe that daikon reduces fevers and rids the body of toxins. Goji berries are filled with powerful antioxidants and are believed to prevent aging. Red dates stimulate the production of white blood cells, which improve immunity and decrease cholesterol in your blood.

I make this soup weekly during the winter months in my slow cooker, but a large stockpot works just as well. The warming ingredients make this an ideal dish to combat chilly weather.

MAKES 6 SERVINGS

2 pounds baby back ribs, ribs separated

Four ½-inch-thick fresh ginger slices

¼ cup dried goji berries

5 red dates

7 cups water

3 small daikon (about 1 pound), peeled and cut diagonally into 2½-inch chunks

Salt

Ground white pepper

1½ cups Spicy Sesame Sauce (page 37) or soy sauce

1. In a large slow cooker, cover the ribs with cold water and bring to a boil, skimming the brown foam that rises to the surface. Add the ginger, goji berries, and red dates to the slow cooker and cover with the water. Cook on high for 4 hours.

2. Add the daikon and more water, if needed, to keep the ingredients covered with liquid. Cook for another 3 hours, or until the ribs are tender. Season with salt and pepper to taste.

3. Divide the broth, ribs, and daikon equally among six shallow bowls. Serve with the Spicy Sesame Sauce on the side.

creamy broccoli soup

During the Cultural Revolution, dairy products were luxury items. Only privileged people, like party members, could buy butter, milk, and yogurt at special shops, but soy was common. For years it was our main source of protein. Now that I have a choice, I still prefer soy over dairy, perhaps because it reminds me of my childhood.

When shopping for broccoli, look for sturdy, dark green spears with tight buds. Avoid any bunches with yellowed florets. Fresh broccoli is an excellent source of beta-carotene, potassium, and calcium. Save the broccoli stems for a stir-fry.

MAKES 6 SERVINGS

2 tablespoons unsalted butter

½ cup chopped red onion

2 cups soy milk or low-fat milk

4 cups broccoli florets (from about 2 pounds broccoli)

Salt

Ground white pepper

½ cup plain soy yogurt or dairy yogurt, for garnish

1. Melt the butter in a large pot over medium heat. Add the onion and sauté until softened, about 4 minutes. Stir in the milk, bring to a boil, reduce the heat, and simmer for 4 minutes.

2. Cook the broccoli florets in rapidly boiling salted water until tender, about 5 minutes. Drain in a colander and rinse under cold water to stop the cooking and set the bright green color.

3. Add the broccoli to the milk mixture and blend with an immersion blender, or transfer to a blender and purée. Return the soup to the saucepan and cook until heated through. Season to taste with salt and pepper. Divide the soup equally among six bowls. Garnish each serving with a dollop of yogurt. Serve hot.

chicken soup with coconut and lemongrass

Last summer, I took my son back to China. In three weeks we visited five cities, including Shangri-La. In addition to experiencing its rich history and culture, we sampled food from all over the world. On our last day there, we rode horses down an ancient tea trade route and stopped at a three-table restaurant that served us a Thai coconut soup.

This rejuvenating chicken soup is my invention after our memorable visit to Shangri-La. To further reduce the fat content I sometimes replace half of the coconut milk with soy milk. This soup reheats nicely, but keep an eye on it, as coconut milk curdles if it cooks for too long.

MAKES 6 SERVINGS

4 lemongrass stalks

2 cups Healthy Homemade Chicken Stock (page 50) or store-bought chicken stock

1 pound boneless, skinless chicken breasts, cut into ½-inch pieces

2 cups fresh or frozen corn kernels

¼ cup fresh lime juice

One 13.5- or 14-ounce can reduced-fat, unsweetened coconut milk

1½ teaspoons fish sauce, or more as needed

1 fresh red chile pepper, minced, for garnish

¼ cup chopped fresh cilantro leaves, for garnish

1. Discard the tough outer leaves of the lemongrass and trim off the root ends. Using only the bottom 6 inches of the stalk, cut the lemongrass into 1-inch pieces from the root end. Discard the remainder.

2. Bring the stock and lemongrass to a boil in a large pot. Add the chicken and corn kernels and return to a boil. Reduce the heat and simmer for 5 minutes, or until the chicken is cooked through. Discard the lemongrass.

3. Stir in the lime juice and coconut milk and bring to a boil. Stir in fish sauce to taste, and remove the pot from the heat. Divide the soup equally among six bowls. Garnish with the chile and cilantro, and serve immediately.

soup of harmony

Black beans are a favorite in China. They are believed to stimulate blood circulation. Chickpeas, a popular ingredient from the Middle East, are a good source of folic acid, fiber, and complex proteins. In this dish I flavor the black beans with jalapeños to enhance their yang, and cook the chickpeas in white tea to enrich their yin.

By pouring light chickpeas and dark black bean purées into shallow soup bowls, side by side, a pattern resembling the yin-yang symbol is created. The design reflects the harmony of the flavors in the dish. The lovely presentation makes it an ideal dish to serve when entertaining.

MAKES 6 SERVINGS

One 15-ounce can black beans

2 cups brewed white or green tea
(see page 15)

3 tablespoons olive oil

1 jalapeño chile, seeded and chopped

2 green onions, white and green parts,
finely chopped

One 15-ounce can chickpeas

2 garlic cloves, minced

1 tablespoon fresh lemon juice

Salt

Freshly ground black pepper

Vegetable stock or water, as needed

1. Drain and rinse the black beans. Reserve 3 beans for garnish. Place the remaining beans, 1 cup of the tea, 4½ teaspoons of the oil, the jalapeño, and green onions in a food processor or blender. Process until puréed, then transfer to a large measuring cup or other container with a pouring spout. Add a little vegetable stock or water if the soup is too thick. Rinse out the food processor or blender.

2. Drain and rinse the chickpeas. Reserve 3 chickpeas for garnish. Place the remaining chickpeas, garlic, lemon juice, the remaining 1 cup tea, and the remaining 4½ teaspoons oil in a food processor or blender. Process until puréed, then transfer to a large measuring cup or other container with a pouring spout.

(continued)

3. Season both puréed soups with salt and pepper to taste. Slowly pour the soups simultaneously into the opposite sides of a large serving bowl. Using a spoon, gently push the edge of the black bean soup to form an *S* shape. The result should resemble the yin-yang symbol. Garnish with the reserved black beans placed at the center of the chickpea soup and the reserved chickpeas in the center of the black bean soup.

COOKING WITH AN ASIAN ACCENT

miso soup with tofu and noodles

The first time I took my young son to Japan, he had yet to develop an appreciation for sushi. When our hosts took us to a restaurant, he ignored the array of sushi, cupped a warm bowl of miso soup in his little hands like the other boys, happily inhaled the aromatic steam, and sipped the broth. After we returned home, he asked me to make him that "delicious soup from Japan." I added noodles to make it a complete meal, which has become one of his favorites.

Fresh udon noodles work best in this dish, but if you can't find them, any fresh linguine or wide rice noodles will do.

MAKES 4 SERVINGS

½ pound udon or soba noodles

4 cups Fresh Vegetable Stock (page 51) or store-bought vegetable stock

8 ounces flavor-baked tofu (see page 4), cut into ½-inch cubes

½ cup peeled and thinly sliced carrots

2 tablespoons red miso

3 green onions, white and green parts, thinly sliced

1 tablespoon sesame oil

¼ cup mung bean or soybean sprouts

Low-sodium soy sauce, for serving

1. Cook the noodles according to the package directions. Drain in a colander under cold running water and set aside.

2. Bring the stock to a boil in a large pot. Add the tofu, cooked noodles, and carrots and bring the soup back to a boil. Reduce the heat to low and simmer for 3 minutes.

3. In a small bowl, mash the miso with about ¼ cup of the warm stock until it forms a smooth sauce; then stir the miso sauce into the soup. Turn off the heat.

4. Divide the soup equally among four shallow bowls. Stir in the green onions and sesame oil. Top with the sprouts. Pass the soy sauce for those who desire it. Serve hot.

cream of shrimp soup

A few years ago, my family and I spent Thanksgiving on the coast of North Carolina. Every day we would go to the docks and buy fresh seafood. I fell in love with the shrimp there. This was my contribution to the Thanksgiving dinner with friends. It's my healthy take on classic Western cream-based soups, with my Asian touch of soy creamer. This soup is extremely versatile—you can substitute salmon, mushrooms, or tofu for the shrimp. Serve with whole wheat bread.

MAKES 4 SERVINGS

2 tablespoons unsalted butter

1 small red onion, chopped

⅓ cup all-purpose flour

1½ cups water

1 cup fresh grapefruit juice

1 pound large shrimp, peeled, deveined, and cooked

½ cup white sweet corn kernels

⅔ cup soy creamer or whole milk

1 tablespoon rice vinegar

Salt

Freshly ground black pepper

2 tablespoons chopped fresh dill, for garnish

1. Melt the butter in a saucepan over medium-low heat. Add the onion and cook until fragrant, about 1 minute. Stir in the flour, cook for 1 minute, then pour in the water and grapefruit juice and bring to a boil.

2. Add three-quarters of the shrimp and the corn kernels and return the soup to a boil. Reduce the heat and simmer for 5 minutes. Stir in the soy creamer and vinegar and return to a quick boil. Let the soup cool slightly. Purée in a blender or food processor. Season to taste with salt and pepper.

3. Divide the soup equally aong four bowls. Garnish with the reserved shrimp and the fresh dill.

all about shrimp

ASIANS LOVE SHRIMP, believing that they strengthen the kidneys. It is considered one of the few types of seafood that have a warming (yang) effect on the body.

You can buy large, medium, or small shrimp cooked or uncooked, shelled or unshelled. Unshelled and uncooked shrimp are more flavorful but require more preparation and cooking time. Precooked and shelled shrimp are less tasty but are ideal for a busy cook.

In general, I use shelled cooked shrimp for weeknight dishes to save time, and unshelled uncooked shrimp for weekend meals.

Since fresh shrimp deteriorates in a couple of days, 98 percent of the shrimp sold on the market are prefrozen. Look for shrimp that are firm and free of odor, ideally coming from a clean water source or farm that is free of antibiotics and hormones.

hot and sour shrimp soup

Vary the heat of this classic Thai soup by using different types of chiles, from the mild poblano to the hot-tempered habanero. I prefer even-tempered jalapeños. Be sure not to overcook the shrimp or they will become tough. For a vegetarian version, firm tofu is a delicious alternative to shrimp.

MAKES 6 SERVINGS

2 lemongrass stalks

4 cups Exotic Green Tea Fish Stock (page 52) or store-bought fish or vegetable stock

1 fresh red chile pepper, seeded and cut into thin strips

2 garlic cloves, crushed

1 pound uncooked jumbo shrimp, peeled and deveined

¼ pound fresh oyster mushrooms, sliced

½ cup watercress leaves

2 tablespoons fresh lime juice

4 green onions, white parts only, minced

1½ teaspoons Thai fish sauce, or more as needed

Lime slices, for garnish

Fresh cilantro leaves, for garnish

1. Discard the tough outer leaves of the lemongrass and trim off the root ends. Use only the bottom 6 inches of the stalks. Discard the remainder.

2. Pour the stock into a large pot. Add the lemongrass, chile, and garlic and bring to a boil. Reduce the heat and simmer until fragrant, 3 to 4 minutes.

3. Add the shrimp, mushrooms, watercress leaves, and lime juice and return to a boil. Reduce the heat and cook just until the shrimp turn pink, 3 to 4 minutes. Add the green onions. Season to taste with fish sauce.

4. Divide the soup equally among six bowls and garnish with the lime slices and cilantro. Serve hot.

tomato and crabmeat egg drop soup

In China, eggs symbolize life and rebirth. Like chicken soup in the West, egg drop soup is considered a nurturing comfort food. When I was young I loved helping my grandmother stir the eggs into the hot stock and watching the strands form.

In my version of this classic dish, I have enriched it with crabmeat and fresh cilantro. You can serve it in smaller portions as an appetizer, or as a light meal on its own in larger portions.

MAKES 8 APPETIZERS OR 4 MAIN-COURSE SERVINGS

2 tablespoons extra-virgin olive oil

2 garlic cloves, minced

1 green onion, white and green parts, chopped

3 fresh shiitake mushrooms, cut into 1-inch cubes

Salt

Ground white pepper

2 medium tomatoes, seeded and cut into 2-inch cubes

4 cups Exotic Green Tea Fish Stock (page 52) or store-bought fish or chicken stock

1 cup fresh or thawed frozen crabmeat

2 large organic eggs, well beaten

1 teaspoon sesame oil

Fresh cilantro leaves, for garnish

1. Heat the oil in a large, heavy saucepan over medium-high heat. Add the garlic, green onion, and mushrooms and sauté until fragrant, about 1 minute. Add a pinch of salt and pepper. Add the tomatoes, reduce the heat to medium-low, and cook, stirring, for 2 to 3 minutes.

2. Add the stock and bring to a boil. Add the crabmeat, return to a boil, and immediately turn off the heat. Slowly drizzle in the beaten eggs while stirring the soup in one direction with a chopstick or fork so the eggs form long threads.

3. Stir in the sesame oil. Season with salt and pepper to taste. Divide the soup equally among the bowls. Garnish with the cilantro and serve hot.

miso soup with shrimp wontons and shiitake mushrooms

Back when we lived in Colorado, my family and friends were always thrilled when I served them this soup after we returned from a ski trip.

Traditional miso soup uses dashi as the base. In this variation I use green tea. The wontons, shiitake mushrooms, and miso make this a hearty, one-bowl meal. It will surely warm you up after a cold day.

MAKES 4 SERVINGS

filling

1 cup boiling water

1 tablespoon loose green tea leaves

½ pound large shrimp, peeled, deveined, and finely chopped

¼ pound extra-lean ground pork

⅓ cup minced green onions, white and green parts

2 teaspoons minced fresh ginger

2 garlic cloves, minced

1 tablespoon soy sauce

2 teaspoons sesame oil

⅛ teaspoon ground white pepper

wontons

20 square wonton wrappers or gyoza skins

5 cups water

1 cup thinly sliced fresh shiitake mushroom caps (about 3 ounces)

3 tablespoons red miso

3 green onions, white parts only, very thinly sliced, for garnish

¼ cup julienned red bell pepper, for garnish

1. **TO MAKE THE FILLING:** Pour the boiling water over the tea leaves. Let steep for 5 minutes. Drain, reserving the tea for the broth, and mince the tea leaves. In a large bowl, combine the tea leaves, shrimp, ground pork, green onions, ginger, garlic, soy sauce, sesame oil, and white pepper and mix well.

2. **TO ASSEMBLE THE WONTONS:** Dip the edges of a wonton wrapper in a bowl of cold water. Place about 1 tablespoon of the filling in the center. Bring the two opposite corners together over the filling and pinch the edges together to seal, forming a triangle. Repeat with the remaining wontons and filling. Keep the filled wontons and remaining wrappers covered with damp towels to prevent them from drying out.

3. In a large pot, bring the 5 cups of water and the reserved tea to a boil. Add the mushrooms and bring back to a boil. Reduce the heat and simmer 5 minutes.

4. Add the wontons, stir gently, and boil until the wontons are translucent and float to the top, 3 to 5 minutes.

5. Remove ¼ cup of the soup broth. Add the miso and stir to dissolve it in the broth. Stir the miso mixture back into the soup.

6. Ladle 5 wontons and equal portions of the broth into each of four deep soup bowls. Garnish each with green onions and bell pepper. Serve hot.

NOTE: Wontons freeze well. To freeze, place them on a lightly floured plate, leaving space between the wontons. Put the plate in the freezer. When the wontons are frozen solid, remove them from the plate and seal them in a plastic freezer bag. To cook, drop the frozen wontons into boiling soup and boil them for about 3 minutes longer than fresh ones.

lamb, potato, and carrot stew

According to TCM doctors, lamb is warming in nature. This hearty stew, flavored with chile and turmeric, will enhance blood circulation. The goji berries add an exotic, Asian twist. Beef or chicken are delicious alternatives to lamb.

MAKES 8 SERVINGS

2 teaspoons all-purpose flour

1 teaspoon salt

2 pounds lamb meat, cut into 1½-inch cubes

2 tablespoons extra-virgin olive oil

4 garlic cloves, minced

3 whole red chile peppers, fresh or dried

6 cups water or Healthy Homemade Chicken Stock (page 50) or store-bought chicken stock

2 tablespoons dried goji berries

1 teaspoon ground turmeric

1 teaspoon dried thyme leaves

1 large red onion, cut into 2-inch wedges

4 medium carrots, peeled and cut diagonally into 2-inch-long pieces

½ pound red potatoes, peeled and cut into 1-inch chunks

Salt

Freshly ground black pepper

Dill sprigs, for garnish

1. Combine 1 teaspoon of the flour and ½ teaspoon of the salt in a bowl. Add half the lamb cubes and toss to coat. Heat 1 tablespoon of the oil in a large pot or Dutch oven over medium-high heat. Add the lamb and brown on all sides. Transfer to a plate. Repeat with the remaining flour, salt, and lamb.

2. In the same pot, heat the remaining 1 tablespoon oil and sauté the garlic and chiles until fragrant, about 30 seconds. Add the stock, cooked lamb and juices, goji berries, turmeric, and thyme. Cook, stirring, for 2 minutes.

3. Add the onion and carrots. Cook, stirring, for 2 minutes. Bring to a boil, reduce the heat to a simmer, and cover. Cook for 1 hour. Add the potatoes and cook for 30 minutes more, uncovered, or until the meat is tender and the liquid has thickened. Season with salt and pepper to taste. Garnish with dill sprigs. Serve warm with bread.

hot pot

WHEN I WAS GROWING UP, making a hot pot involved the entire family. My brothers would help my father light the charcoal stove. Mother would put broth in the pot and prepare the dipping sauces while I arranged the ingredients on serving plates.

A hot pot, also called a sand pot, is usually a ceramic pot with a rough, unglazed exterior and a glazed interior. You can find hot pots at Asian grocery stores or online. Broth is boiled in the pot over a small charcoal brazier in the center of the table.

However, I have found it more practical to use a heatproof casserole dish set on an electric hot plate or over a gas or alcohol burner. An electric wok or a fondue set also works well. Once the broth in the hot pot is boiling, everyone cooks his or her own ingredients.

Vegetables only need to be immersed briefly until they are heated through. Tofu, mushrooms, and meat need a little longer, about 1 minute. The broth becomes more flavorful as everyone cooks their food. Toward the end of the meal, the remaining well-seasoned broth is divided and enjoyed. Each person should have a large slotted spoon or chopsticks to move his or her food to and from the hot pot; small, shallow bowls for dipping sauces; and individual bowls.

Since cooking time is short when using a hot pot, all the ingredients must be prepared in advance. Arrange them artistically on the serving plates. Traditionally, diners cook the dipping ingredients for hot pots one at a time. But if you are in a hurry, combine them in a heavy pot and cook them on the stovetop as a stew.

heartwarming hot pot

This is always the featured dish at my Chinese New Year party. Vegetarian meatballs are available in the frozen-food sections of most natural food stores. You can substitute cubed extra-firm tofu, or ground beef, turkey, or chicken meatballs for the vegetarian meatballs.

MAKES 4 SERVINGS

dipping sauce

½ cup red miso

2 tablespoons honey

2 tablespoons sake or white wine

4½ teaspoons toasted sesame oil

1 small green onion, minced

1 fresh red chile pepper, minced

2 tablespoons minced fresh cilantro leaves

dipping ingredients

9 ounces fresh or dried udon or other noodles

One 12-ounce package vegetarian meatballs

½ pound fresh shiitake mushrooms, caps cut into 3-inch-wide strips (stems reserved for the broth)

½ pound butternut or other winter squash, peeled and cubed

½ pound snow peas

broth

4 cups Fresh Vegetable Stock (page 51) or store-bought vegetable stock

2 cups rice milk

½ pound fresh shiitake mushroom stems (reserved from dipping ingredients)

1 cup shelled fresh or frozen edamame (soybeans)

2 tablespoons sliced fresh ginger

2 tablespoons dried goji berries

2 teaspoons sesame oil

Salt

Freshly ground black pepper

1. **TO MAKE THE DIPPING SAUCE:** Combine the ingredients for the dipping sauce in a large bowl. Divide equally among four saucers.

2. **TO PREPARE THE DIPPING INGREDIENTS:** Cook the noodles according to the package directions. Drain and rinse under cold water. Set aside.

(continued)

3. Arrange the cooked noodles, meatballs, mushrooms, squash, and snow peas attractively on a large serving plate.

4. **TO MAKE THE BROTH:** Bring all of the ingredients for the broth except the sesame oil, salt, and pepper to a boil in a metal fondue pot over a lit burner or in an electric wok in the center of the table. If you don't have a large pot, use a smaller one and add more broth and water as the meal progresses.

5. Once the broth is boiling, turn off the heat. Drizzle in the sesame oil and season with salt and pepper to taste. Have each person use a large slotted spoon or chopsticks to select the hot pot ingredients he or she wants to cook and place them in the central cooking pot. Scald a few ingredients at a time. The noodles, squash, and snow peas only need to be heated through. The vegetarian meatballs and mushrooms need a little longer, about 1 minute.

6. Serve the cooked food accompanied by the dipping sauce. Toward the end of the meal, ladle the remaining well-seasoned broth into individual bowls, dividing it equally among the diners.

meaty yang hot pot

Make sure you have the dipping sauce, ingredients, and broth prepared in advance and ready to go. Partially freeze the beef, lamb, and chicken so they can be thinly sliced easily.

This hot pot, packed with meat, ginseng, and tofu, and served with a spicy dipping sauce, will help ward off the winter chill, replenish your *chi*, and boost your yang energy.

MAKES 6 SERVINGS

dipping sauce

¼ cup soy sauce

¼ cup rice vinegar

2 tablespoons oyster sauce

2 tablespoons fresh lemon juice

¼ teaspoon minced fresh red chile pepper

dipping ingredients

½ pound beef flank steak, cut into ⅛-inch-thick slices

¼ pound boneless lean lamb, cut into ⅛-inch-thick slices

½ pound boneless, skinless chicken breasts, cut into 3-inch-wide strips

1 pound firm tofu, cut into 2-inch cubes

1 large onion, cubed

4 green onions, white and green parts, cut into 2-inch lengths

½ pound tender asparagus, cut into 2-inch lengths

broth

5 cups Healthy Homemade Chicken Stock (page 50) or store-bought chicken stock

½ ginseng root or 6 ginseng slices

1. **TO MAKE THE DIPPING SAUCE:** Combine the soy sauce, rice vinegar, oyster sauce, and lemon juice in a small bowl. Divide equally among six dipping bowls. Sprinkle a little of the chile over each bowl.

2. **TO PREPARE THE DIPPING INGREDIENTS:** Arrange the meat, tofu, and vegetables on serving plates.

3. **TO MAKE THE BROTH:** Bring the stock and ginseng to a boil in a large pot over high heat. Carefully transfer the pot to a hot plate on the table, or pour the hot broth into an electric wok or a metal fondue pot over a lit burner adjusted

(continued)

to the highest setting. If you don't have a large pot, use a smaller one and add broth and water as the meal progresses.

4. Once the broth is boiling, have each person use a large slotted spoon or chopsticks to select the hot pot ingredients he or she wants to cook and place them in the central cooking pot. Scald a few ingredients at a time for about 1 minute, eating and dipping as the food is cooked. Do not overcook.

5. Toward the end of the meal, ladle the remaining well-seasoned broth into individual bowls, dividing it equally among the diners.

pumpkin-seafood pot

Every autumn when I see pumpkins in stores, they always remind me of a favorite Chinese dish made with winter melon and inspire me to cook this dish.

With its sweet, neutral flavor, pumpkin is thought to combat cold season infections and stimulate the digestive system. The pumpkin is used as a tureen in this Western take on the Chinese classic. Be sure to use a sugar pumpkin, not a tough, stringy jack-o'-lantern.

MAKES 6 SERVINGS

1 medium baking pumpkin (8 to 10 pounds)

2 tablespoons extra-virgin olive oil

1 pound small white onions, cut into ½-inch chunks

½ pound large fresh or uncooked frozen shrimp, peeled and deveined

½ pound sea scallops

5 cups Exotic Green Tea Fish Stock (page 52) or store-bought vegetable stock or fish stock

4 pieces ginseng, sliced (optional)

6 fresh or dried shiitake mushrooms

4 ounces fresh or frozen crabmeat

1 medium zucchini, cut into 1-inch pieces

1 medium yellow squash, cut into 1-inch pieces

Salt

Freshly ground black pepper

4 sprigs fresh cilantro and/or basil, for garnish

1. Rinse and dry the outside of the pumpkin. Remove the top with a knife. Scoop out and discard the seeds and membranes. Carve a decorative motif on the skin without piercing the pumpkin. With a knife make zigzag cuts around the rim.

2. In a large pot, heat the oil over medium-high heat until hot. Add the onions and cook until golden. Add the shrimp and scallops and stir-fry until the shrimp turn pink and the scallops are opaque, 1 to 2 minutes. Add the stock, ginseng, and mushrooms and bring to a boil. Reduce the heat to low, cover, and simmer for 5 minutes.

(continued)

3. Place the pumpkin shell upright in a heatproof dish and place the dish on a rack in a steamer large enough to hold the pumpkin. Pour the hot soup, crabmeat, zucchini, and squash into the pumpkin. Cover and steam over briskly boiling water until the pumpkin flesh softens, 25 to 30 minutes.

4. Transfer the pumpkin to a serving platter. Season the soup with salt and pepper to taste and garnish with the cilantro and/or basil. To serve, spoon out the stew along with some of the pumpkin flesh for each serving.

all about scallops

THERE ARE SEVERAL TYPES OF SCALLOPS: fresh sea and bay scallops as well as dried sea and bay scallops. The larger fresh sea scallops are good for grilling or pan-frying, while the smaller and more delicate bay scallops are better for soups, stews, and stir-fries.

Like shrimp, the larger the scallops, the more expensive they will be.

Look for fresh wild scallops that are firm and free of fishy or sour smells. In a pinch, quick-frozen ones are good substitutes.

tofu hot pot

When I was young my brothers and I would fight to place a plate of tofu on the windowsill on cold nights, as my family did not own a freezer. The next morning I would get up early so I could "harvest" the frozen tofu before them. Now I always have a few pieces of frozen tofu in my freezer.

Freezing and thawing the tofu gives it a firmer, chewier texture, and makes it more porous, so that it soaks up the soup's flavors.

According to TCM, both bok choy and Napa cabbage, as well as tofu, cleanse and stimulate the digestive system, making this an ideal dish for spring.

MAKES 6 SERVINGS

One 16-ounce package extra-firm tofu

½ pound dried rice stick noodles or bean thread noodles

5 cups boiling water

1 cup low-sodium soy sauce

1½ cups Chile-Garlic Sauce (page 27)

1 cup snow peas

½ pound baby bok choy or Napa cabbage, cut into 4-inch pieces

1 red bell pepper, seeded and cut into 2-inch pieces

1 yellow bell pepper, seeded and cut into 2-inch pieces

broth

6 cups Fresh Vegetable Stock (page 51) or store-bought vegetable stock

2 tablespoons rice wine or dry sherry

½ ginseng root or 4 ginseng slices

2 teaspoons salt

1. Freeze the tofu overnight, then thaw it in the package in the refrigerator. Squeeze out excess water and cut it into 2-inch cubes.

2. Soak the noodles in the boiling water until soft, 8 to 10 minutes. Drain and set aside.

3. Divide the tofu, noodles, and soy sauce equally among six soup bowls. Divide the Chile-Garlic Sauce equally among six small saucers. Arrange the vegetables on a large serving plate.

4. **TO MAKE THE BROTH:** Bring the stock, rice wine, ginseng, and salt to a boil in a large pot over high heat. Carefully transfer the pot to a hot plate on the table, or pour the hot broth into an electric wok or a metal fondue pot over a lit burner adjusted to the highest setting. If you don't have a large pot, use a smaller one and add more broth and water as the meal progresses.

5. Once the broth is boiling, have each person use a large slotted spoon or chopsticks to select the hot pot ingredients he or she wants to cook and place them in the central cooking pot. Scald a few ingredients at a time for about 1 minute (tofu takes a little longer), eating and dipping as the food is cooked.

6. Toward the end, ladle the remaining well-seasoned broth into individual bowls, dividing it equally among the diners.

NOTE: If you are pressed for time or don't have the equipment, combine all the broth ingredients in a large pot and bring to a boil. Reduce the heat to medium-low. Add the tofu, vegetables, and noodles. Cover and simmer for 4 to 5 minutes, or until the vegetables and noodles soften. Garnish with 1 tablespoon sesame oil and 2 minced green onions.

Combine the sauce ingredients in one large bowl; add one-third of the sauce to the broth, then ladle the rest into shallow bowls, one per person, as a dipping sauce. Serve hot and enjoy.

east
meets
west
salads

While salads of fresh, raw vegetables are common in Western cooking, I rarely had them when growing up.

Asians prefer to cook their greens, in part because tap water in many parts of Asia is contaminated, and produce can come from unclean sources. During my childhood, vegetables were sold in mud-covered piles in the street markets. It was a tremendous ordeal to clean them every day.

When I arrived in the United States, I was delightfully surprised to find I could drink water straight from the tap, and when I found I could buy prewashed vegetables, I was ecstatic! By merging the traditional Eastern flavors with Western ideas, I developed these recipes that are quick, adventurous, unusual, and nutritious. Many ingredients used in these salads are easy to come by, yet each contributes its own special flavor or texture—be it spicy, sweet, tangy, juicy, crunchy, or chewy.

By pairing cooling vegetables with warming spices, meats, and nuts, you can quickly produce a well-balanced meal with delicious tastes and therapeutic effects. With combinations of vegetables, whole grains, and a variety of meat, tofu, seafood, or nuts, you have ample antioxidants, omega-3 fatty acids, vitamins, and protein.

To help beat summer's heat, try cooling salads such as Snow Pea and Crabmeat Salad (page 86), Papaya, Grapefruit, and Avocado Salad (page 90), or Three-Melon Salad (page 93). What could be a better way to enjoy the fresh produce from your garden or the farmers' market? These dishes also nicely complement any meal cooked on the grill.

The hearty, colorful, warm yang salads, such as Couscous-Fennel Salad with Oranges and Almonds (page 96), Smoked Salmon Pasta Salad with Grapefruit Dressing (page 103), and Black Tea–Crusted Tofu and Shrimp with Baby Greens (page 98), incorporate authentic Asian flavors with popular Western ingredients. These exotic creations will lighten your winter table, and delight your eyes and taste buds.

The combinations of vegetables, grains, and lean proteins—tofu, nuts, and seafood—are endless. They make healthful, well-balanced meals always within reach.

snow pea and crabmeat salad

According to TCM, both snow peas and crabmeat are sweet and cooling in nature. Together they stimulate the sense of taste, relieve fatigue, and help heal heat rash. Because of its cooling effects, this salad complements almost any type of food cooked on the outdoor grill. Use fresh, tender snow peas.

MAKES 4 SERVINGS

½ pound lump crabmeat, picked over to remove any shells

1 Thai chile pepper, finely minced

1 green onion, minced

4½ teaspoons fresh lemon juice

1 tablespoon soy sauce

1 ½ teaspoons rice wine

1 pound tender snow peas, trimmed and cut into 1-inch lengths

¼ cup honey-roasted chopped nuts of your choosing

1. Combine the crabmeat, chile, green onion, lemon juice, soy sauce, and rice wine in a bowl and set aside.

2. Bring a large pot of salted water to a boil. Add the snow peas and blanch them until they turn bright green, about 1 minute. Drain and rinse under cold water until chilled.

3. Toss the snow peas with the crabmeat mixture in the bowl. Top with the nuts and serve.

spinach salad with smoked salmon and walnuts

This is one of my medicinal dishes. It contains ingredients that my Chinese doctor mother used to encourage me to consume. Spinach and tomato lubricate aerobic dryness, while walnuts and salmon sharpen the mind and replenish the *chi*. Enjoy this delicious salad while knowing it is also so good for you.

MAKES 4 SERVINGS

2 cups baby spinach leaves

1 red tomato, sliced into wedges

1 yellow tomato, sliced into wedges

1 cup fresh blueberries

½ pound smoked salmon, cut into ½-inch pieces

3 tablespoons walnut oil or extra-virgin olive oil

2 tablespoons balsamic vinegar

Salt

Freshly ground black pepper

½ cup candied walnuts (see page 88) or store-bought nuts

1. In a large salad bowl, toss together the spinach, tomatoes, blueberries, smoked salmon, oil, vinegar, and salt and pepper to taste.

2. Top with the walnuts and serve.

how to make candied nuts

MAKES ABOUT 2½ CUPS

1 cup light brown muscovado sugar

3 tablespoons water

2 teaspoons pure vanilla extract

2 cups chopped walnuts or pecans

These candied nuts lend a delightful Western touch to many Asian dishes. Muscovado sugar is also called "Barbados sugar." This unrefined brown sugar gets its strong molasses flavor from the juice of the sugarcane and is ideal for baking. If you can't find it, substitute regular brown sugar. "Wrinkly" nuts like pecans and walnuts work the best (smooth nuts like peanuts don't pick up as much of the melted sugar). Double or triple the recipe as needed and use the nuts in desserts or sprinkle them on top of salads. They make for a great snack when you need a quick burst of energy.

1. Preheat the oven to 350°F (177°C).

2. Bring the sugar, water, and vanilla to a boil in a saucepan. Fold the nuts into the sugar mixture, using a spatula, and coat thoroughly. Spread the nuts out on a baking sheet and bake for 10 minutes. Let cool, then transfer to a sealed container and store at room temperature for up to 1 week.

chickpea-avocado salad with spicy sesame sauce

I had my first avocado after I came to the United States in my early twenties. It reminded me of tofu's mild versatility. After learning its health benefits, I started to incorporate it into my cooking and was pleasantly surprised by how well it pairs with the spicy Asian dressing in this salad.

Whenever I come home from a long trip, I make this salad to give my body a healthy boost. Avocado contains heart-healthy fat and is high in fiber, potassium, and vitamins C, K, folate, and B6. Chickpeas are a great source of protein. For a hearty meal, serve the salad with whole-grain bread.

MAKES 4 SERVINGS

2 cups cooked or canned chickpeas, rinsed and drained

1 small red onion, finely chopped

1 small red bell pepper, seeded and diced

12 black olives, such as Kalamata, pitted and halved

2 avocados, pitted, peeled, and quartered

½ cup Spicy Sesame Sauce (page 37)

2 tablespoons chopped fresh mint leaves, for garnish

1. Place the chickpeas in a salad bowl. Add the onion, bell pepper, and olives. Arrange the avocados on top.

2. Divide the salad equally among four plates. Spoon the sauce over the salad and garnish with the mint just before serving.

papaya, grapefruit, and avocado salad

Throughout Southeast Asia, many dishes use banana leaves as plates, making for a striking, vibrant presentation. Since banana leaves can be hard to come by in the United States, I often substitute lettuce leaves.

Serve this cooling salad as a late-spring starter or side dish. To make it a main course, add smoked salmon, sautéed shrimp, or grilled flavored tofu. The sweet papaya and tart grapefruit meld with the creamy avocado to make a wonderfully complementary combination.

MAKES 6 SERVINGS

salad

2 medium pink grapefruits, halved and segmented, juice reserved

2 medium avocados, halved, pitted, peeled, and sliced

1 large papaya, peeled, halved, seeded, and thinly sliced

Banana leaves or lettuce leaves, for lining the platter

dressing

2 tablespoons extra-virgin olive oil

2 tablespoons white wine vinegar

Freshly ground black pepper

2 tablespoons jarred capers, packed in brine; do not rinse, for garnish

1. **TO PREPARE THE SALAD:** Arrange the grapefruit segments, avocados, and papaya attractively on a large serving platter lined with the banana leaves.

2. **TO MAKE THE DRESSING:** Whisk together the oil and vinegar in a small bowl. Season to taste with pepper. Mix the reserved grapefruit juice into the dressing.

3. Drizzle the dressing over the salad. Garnish with the capers and serve.

shrimp-mango salad

Every time I see a mango, I feel a sense of amused nostalgia. During the Cultural Revolution, the communist leader Chairman Mao used it in his political campaigns. There was a picture hanging in our classroom that showed him giving a golden mango in a glass case to a group of workers.

Wuhan, the city where I grew up, is in central inland China, so I never touched a real mango until I came to the United States. You could say that mangoes have a special place in my memory. I love their aromatic smell and sweet taste and have incorporated them into many of my recipes, like this one.

MAKES 4 SERVINGS

½ pound uncooked shrimp, peeled and deveined

¼ cup Essential Thai Peanut Sauce (page 41)

2 tablespoons extra-virgin olive oil or canola oil

4 garlic cloves, chopped

1 cup snap peas

2 green onions, green and white parts, cut into 2-inch lengths

2 cups mixed salad greens

2 mangoes, peeled, pitted, and sliced

¼ cup Candied Nuts (page 000) or store-bought nuts

1. Mix the shrimp and sauce together in a bowl. Cover and refrigerate for 15 minutes or overnight.

2. Heat the oil in a nonstick skillet. Add the garlic and sauté until fragrant. Add the shrimp and stir-fry until they turn opaque, about 3 minutes. Add the peas and green onions and stir-fry until the peas turn bright green and the green onions begin to soften, about 1 minute.

3. Divide the salad greens among four large plates, placing them to one side of each plate. Arrange the mango slices in a fan shape opposite the salad greens on the plates. Spoon the shrimp mixture onto the salad leaves, top with the nuts, and serve.

three-melon salad

As a little girl I loved following my grandmother to the night market on hot summer evenings to pick out melons. I would follow her lead, smelling and thumping the melons with my little fingers even though I didn't know what I was doing.

Later I learned that selecting a perfect melon doesn't have to be a daunting task. Let your eyes and nose guide you. The most fragrant ones tend to be the ripest. Choose melons that feel heavy, with no cracks or soft spots. Small, heavy melons usually have more flesh in proportion to the seeds.

This refreshing, cooling salad nicely accompanies grilled meat or seafood. For a lovely presentation, serve it in a large glass bowl.

MAKES 6 SERVINGS

1 cup ripe cantaloupe balls

1 cup ripe honeydew melon balls

1 cup seedless watermelon balls

½ cup brewed green tea (see page 15)

3 tablespoons honey

1½ teaspoons fresh lemon juice

3 tablespoons chopped fresh mint leaves, for garnish

1. Place the melon balls into a bowl.

2. In a small saucepan, mix together the tea, honey, and lemon juice. Bring to a boil, then set aside to cool.

3. Just before serving, spoon the sauce over the melon balls, mix gently, and garnish with the mint.

wild rice with cranberries and pine nuts

In this dish, I added the Eastern elements of white tea and shiitake mushrooms to complement the traditional American flavors of wild rice and cranberries. The mushrooms bring a delicately savory flavor to the rice. Although I cook this dish year-round as a delicious side dish, it's become a popular stuffing for poultry or pork tenderloin for my holiday parties. Its marriage of cranberries and pine nuts makes it a healthy alternative to ordinary bread stuffing. For your next holiday party, try this as a stuffing!

MAKES 4 TO 6 SERVINGS

2 cups wild rice

4 cups cold water

3 white tea bags

¼ cup extra-virgin olive oil

4 garlic cloves, minced

1 cup fresh oyster or shiitake mushrooms, stemmed, caps minced

3 medium carrots, cut into ¼-inch cubes (about 2 cups)

½ cup minced onion

2 celery stalks, cut into ¼-inch cubes

1 cup fresh orange juice

1 cup dried cranberries

2 tablespoons chopped fresh flat-leaf parsley

Salt

Freshly ground black pepper

½ cup pine nuts or sliced almonds, toasted (see page 99), for garnish

1. Rinse the rice thoroughly with cold water. Place the rice, water, and tea bags in a 6-quart saucepan and bring to a boil. Remove the tea bags and discard. Reduce the heat to medium-low and let simmer, partially covered, until the rice has puffed and most of the liquid is absorbed, 55 to 60 minutes.

2. Preheat the oven to 325°F (165°C). Heat a wok or nonstick skillet over

medium-high heat. Add the oil and swirl the pan to coat. Add the garlic and sauté until fragrant, about 30 seconds. Add the mushrooms and stir-fry for 1 minute. Add the carrots, onion, and celery and stir-fry until the vegetables are tender, about 2 minutes.

3. Stir in the rice, orange juice, cranberries, and parsley and season to taste with salt and pepper. Toss to mix well.

4. Pour the rice mixture into a 13 x 9-inch baking dish. Cover with aluminum foil and bake until heated through and the liquid has evaporated, about 30 minutes. Garnish with the toasted pine nuts just before serving.

TIPS: While the rice simmers, prepare the other ingredients. If using this dish as a stuffing, it can be made ahead. Pour the rice mixture into the baking pan, cover, and refrigerate. Bake just before serving.

couscous-fennel salad with oranges and almonds

Years ago, while I sailed down the Nile, I had a meal at a small restaurant. It was the first time I'd eaten couscous. Since then I've fallen in love with it. Couscous is easy and versatile to cook with, and it has found its way into many of my dishes.

In this dish I combine hearty couscous and chickpeas with fresh greens and dress them in a tangy, orange-soy dressing. It is a meal in itself, perfect for every season.

MAKES 4 SERVINGS

1 cup fresh orange juice

½ cup couscous

¾ cup (½ can) canned chickpeas, rinsed and drained

½ cup minced fennel bulbs

1 green onion, green and white parts, cut on the diagonal into 2-inch slices

½ cup Green Tea–Orange Sauce (page 30)

1 large navel orange, peeled, segmented, and cut into bite-size pieces

¼ cup dried cranberries, for garnish

¼ cup sliced almonds, toasted (see page 99), for garnish

1. In a 2-quart saucepan over medium-high heat, bring the orange juice to a boil. Stir in the couscous. Cover the saucepan immediately and remove from the heat. Let stand for 5 minutes. Fluff with a fork.

2. In a large salad bowl, combine the couscous, chickpeas, fennel, and green onion with the sauce and toss to coat. Stir in the orange pieces.

3. Divide the salad equally among four plates, garnish with the cranberries and almonds, and serve.

thai-style cabbage salad

Napa cabbage is also called Chinese cabbage. This pale green and yellow oblong vegetable is beloved throughout Asia, and is low in calories and rich in antioxidants and fiber.

Chinese frequently stir-fry cabbage, but it wasn't until I visited Thailand that I encountered Napa cabbage in a salad, paired with peanuts and chile peppers. I've modified the recipe by blanching the cabbage in tea, giving it a unique, aromatic flavor. The leftover broth makes a wonderful soup base.

MAKES 4 TO 6 SERVINGS

4 cups brewed white or green tea (see page 15)

1 small Napa cabbage, shredded

2 tablespoons extra-virgin olive oil

1 dried or fresh red chile pepper, seeded and finely cut into strips

3 garlic cloves, minced

2 fresh or dried shiitake mushrooms, finely cut into strips

¼ cup Essential Thai Peanut Sauce (page 41)

¼ cup roasted peanuts

1. Place the tea in a saucepan and bring to a boil. Add the cabbage and boil for 2 minutes. Drain thoroughly. Place the cabbage in a serving bowl.

2. Heat a wok or nonstick skillet over medium-high heat. Add the oil and swirl the pan to coat. Add the chile, garlic, and mushrooms and stir-fry until the mushroom strips are browned and crisp. Set aside.

3. In a large serving bowl, combine the sauce with the salad and toss well. Sprinkle with the fried mushroom mixture and nuts and serve.

black tea–crusted tofu and shrimp with baby greens

This dish was inspired by my visit to a tea farm in southeast China. I ate dinner at the house of a farmer who served me homemade tofu, vegetables, and fruit from her garden. It was a simple yet memorable meal. The differences are she used river shrimp and stir-fried the vegetables. Here I use small salad shrimp and serve the tofu atop a fresh salad. In this dish, the smooth tofu absorbs the Spicy Sesame Sauce. The pears add a sweet note and the sesame seeds provide a bit of nutty crunch.

MAKES 4 SERVINGS

One 16-ounce package extra-firm tofu

2 tablespoons olive oil

2 teaspoons loose black tea or contents of 2 tea bags

4½ teaspoons black sesame seeds

⅛ teaspoon salt

4 cups baby green salad mix

2 Asian pears or Bosc pears, cubed

1 cup cherry tomatoes (about 8 ounces), halved

¼ pound precooked shrimp

½ cup Spicy Sesame Sauce (page 37)

½ cup toasted nuts (see page 99)

1. Place the tofu on a flat surface and pat firmly with paper towels to remove as much water as possible. Cut the tofu horizontally into 2 large pieces, then cut those in half vertically, and then into quarters; you will have 8 equal cubes.

2. Heat a wok or large, nonstick skillet over medium-high heat. Add the oil and swirl to coat. Add the tea leaves, sesame seeds, and salt and sauté until fragrant, about 30 seconds.

3. Lay the tofu slices on top of the tea leaf mixture and pan-fry until golden brown, about 3 minutes. Using a spatula, turn the tofu and pan-fry the other side until golden brown, about 3 minutes. Drain the tofu on paper towels. Cut into bite-size chunks.

4. Toss the salad greens, pears, tomatoes, and shrimp together in a large serving bowl. Arrange the tofu pieces over the salad and spoon the sauce on top. Sprinkle with the nuts and serve.

how to toast nuts

YOU CAN TOAST NUTS in the oven or in a skillet. The toasting time will vary depending on the size of the nuts. Larger nuts, such as walnuts, pecans, or almonds take longer than smaller nuts such as peanuts, pine nuts, or macadamia nuts. Once cool, store them in an airtight container.

in the oven: Preheat the oven to 350°F (177°C). Arrange the nuts in a single layer on a baking sheet. Place in the middle rack of the oven and toast for 10 to 15 minutes, until nuts turn golden brown. Stir a few times during toasting so the nuts in the middle toast as quickly as the ones at the edges of the pan.

on the stovetop: Sauté the nuts in a skillet over medium-high heat for 3 to 5 minutes, stirring frequently, until the nuts start to turn golden brown. Transfer to a plate and cool.

beef, orange, and spinach salad

TCM believes that cooling spinach aids digestion. Warming garlic and ginger invigorate the taste buds. The combination has a harmonizing effect.

This is one of my go-to dishes on a busy weeknight. If you have some leftover grilled steak, you can put together this salad in less than ten minutes. Or, buy some thinly sliced organic roast beef at the deli counter.

MAKES 4 TO 6 SERVINGS

3 oranges, peeled and segmented

½ pound fresh young spinach leaves

¼ cup chopped fresh chives

3 garlic cloves, finely minced

1 teaspoon minced fresh ginger

1 tablespoon Savory Green Tea Oil (page 42) or extra-virgin olive oil

1 tablespoon rice vinegar

1 pound steak, grilled and thinly sliced

1. In a large salad bowl, gently mix together the oranges, spinach, chives, garlic, ginger, oil, and rice vinegar.

2. Divide the salad among four to six serving plates. Top with the sliced steak and serve.

chicken pasta salad with papaya seed dressing

This salad was inspired by a papaya-chicken salad I ate at a beach resort in Southeast Asia. I wrote down the recipe on a napkin during the meal. I have modified the dish by adding pasta.

The seeds of small papayas, with their light, peppery flavor, are edible. They add a crunchy texture to dressings while also serving as a natural meat tenderizer. To save time, use organic chicken from the deli.

MAKES 4 SERVINGS

dressing

3 garlic cloves, peeled and minced

3 tablespoons minced fresh chives

2 tablespoons seeds of a small papaya

½ cup fresh orange juice

2 tablespoons extra-virgin olive oil

1 tablespoon balsamic vinegar

Salt

salad

8 ounces bow-tie pasta

½ small red bell pepper, seeded and cut into matchstick-size strips

½ small yellow bell pepper, seeded and cut into matchstick-size strips

6 ounces roasted chicken, cut into long thin strips

Salt

Freshly ground black pepper

1. **TO MAKE THE DRESSING:** Combine all of the dressing ingredients in a jar, cover with a lid, and shake to blend. Store in the refrigerator for 30 minutes before using. The dressing will keep in the refrigerator for 3 days. Shake again before using.

2. Cook the pasta according to the package directions. Drain and rinse with cold water to prevent sticking.

3. **TO ASSEMBLE THE SALAD:** Place the pasta and bell peppers in a serving bowl. Toss thoroughly with the dressing, then add the chicken, and toss again. Season to taste with salt and pepper, if needed. Divide the salad equally among four plates and serve.

smoked salmon pasta salad with grapefruit dressing

A warming and hearty pasta salad with smoked salmon is brightened with a burst of citrus flavor. The complex carbohydrates and protein in this dish will provide you with long-lasting fuel for a busy day. The sweet-spicy dressing complements the distinguished smoked salmon, enlivening the mild pasta. If you have a busy week ahead, cook the pasta in advance. It can be refrigerated for up to three days. When you are ready to assemble the dish, simply rinse the pasta under warm water.

MAKES 6 SERVINGS

dressing

¼ cup grapefruit juice

2 tablespoons extra-virgin olive oil

1½ teaspoons honey

2 garlic cloves, minced

3 tablespoons minced fresh basil leaves

1 teaspoon minced fresh ginger

1 teaspoon minced jalapeño chile

⅛ teaspoon salt

salad

12 ounces whole wheat penne

½ cup chopped sun-dried tomatoes, preferably oil-packed

2 ripe yellow or red tomatoes, cut into wedges

6 ounces smoked salmon, cut into 1-inch squares

Salt

Freshly ground black pepper

1. **TO MAKE THE DRESSING:** Combine all of the dressing ingredients in a jar, cover with a lid, and shake well to blend. Set aside.

2. Cook the pasta according to the package directions. Drain and rinse with cold water to prevent sticking. Transfer to a serving bowl.

3. **TO ASSEMBLE THE SALAD:** Stir in the dried and fresh tomatoes and the salmon. Toss with the dressing, and season to taste with salt and pepper. Divide equally among six plates. Serve warm.

global
wraps

When I was four years old my grandmother gave me my first pair of chopsticks, tied together at the top with a rubber band.

This was a common practice for teaching children to use chopsticks in China. That day, Grandma served rice noodles for lunch. Even with the rubber bands in place, the noodles kept slipping from my chopsticks. I grew frustrated. Finally, I rolled up my sleeves, grabbed the noodles with my hands, and stuffed them into my mouth.

Eating with my hands always brings back fond memories of my childhood. It remains one of my favorite ways to enjoy dumplings, spring rolls, and wraps, filled with an assortment of flavorful ingredients and accompanied by versatile dipping sauces. As a food writer, I enjoy experimenting with just about anything soft and pliable that can be used as wrappers—tortillas, lettuce leaves, blanched cabbage leaves, and even leaves harvested from my grapevines.

Wraps are a truly international cuisine, appearing in some form in many cultures, ranging from the ubiquitous egg rolls and burritos to Middle Eastern pita bread and exotic lettuce cups.

Wrapped foods make for creative, healthy meals. You can also serve them in smaller portions as appetizers. Feel free to create your own casual and seasonal roll-ups to suit your time, place, and mood. Perhaps it's the child in all of us that makes eating food without utensils a fun experience—an occasion for taking food into our own hands.

crispy spring rolls with spicy tofu, vegetables, and toasted nuts

I love visiting Buddhist temples in Asia, not for religious reasons but because I enjoy the food served in their restaurants. This recipe was inspired by the fried vegetarian spring rolls I ate at the Shaolin Temple.

While I enjoy crispy fried spring rolls, I dislike their high calorie count and the mess from deep-frying them. I found that by brushing a little olive oil on these rolls and broiling them in the oven, they came out just as crispy and delicious.

MAKES 12 SPRING ROLLS

2 tablespoons olive oil or canola oil

2 teaspoons minced fresh ginger

2 garlic cloves, minced

One 8-ounce package Thai- or teriyaki-flavored tofu, cut into ½-inch cubes

1 cup (about 3 ounces) finely chopped fresh oyster mushrooms

½ cup finely diced carrot

½ cup finely diced water chestnuts

2 tablespoons tamari sauce

¾ cup toasted peanuts or walnuts (see page 99), coarsely chopped, ¼ cup reserved for garnish

2 green onions, minced

1 teaspoon sesame oil

Twelve 8-inch round dried rice paper wrappers (see page 12)

1 head Boston or Bibb lettuce, leaves washed and separated

Lime-Soy-Ginger Sauce (page 32), for serving

1. Heat a wok or nonstick skillet over medium heat. Add the olive oil and swirl to coat. Add the ginger and garlic and stir-fry until fragrant, about 30 seconds. Add the tofu and mushrooms and stir-fry for 2 minutes. Add the carrot and water chestnuts and stir-fry until heated through, about 30 seconds.

(continued)

2. Add the tamari sauce. Cook, stirring occasionally, until the vegetables are heated through, about 2 minutes. Stir in the nuts, green onions, and sesame oil and toss to combine. Remove from the heat.

3. Fill a medium bowl with warm water. Dip one of the wrappers in the water for 15 seconds, or until softened. Carefully transfer to a dry work surface.

4. Arrange 2 to 3 tablespoons of the filling in an even horizontal mound just below the center of the wrapper. Roll up the rice paper to form a tight cylinder, folding in the sides about halfway. Assemble the remaining spring rolls in the same manner. Cover the finished rolls with a damp cloth to prevent them from drying out.

5. Preheat the broiler. Lightly coat a large nonstick baking sheet with cooking spray. Arrange the spring rolls in a single layer on the baking sheet, leaving a little space between them. Lightly coat the rolls with cooking spray.

6. Broil the rolls until lightly browned and crisp, 10 to 13 minutes. Using tongs or a spatula, turn the rolls over and continue to broil for another 8 to 10 minutes.

7. Serve each roll wrapped in a lettuce leaf garnished with nuts, and accompanied by the Lime-Soy-Ginger Sauce.

crisp apple-chicken spring rolls

The difference between spring rolls and egg rolls is that egg rolls are always cooked (usually deep-fried), while spring rolls can be served cooked or raw. Another difference is the skin: egg roll skins are made with wheat flour and eggs, while spring roll wrappers are made of rice flour and water. Spring rolls also tend to be filled with fresh vegetables, fruits, and seasonings, while egg rolls usually have meat as part of the filling.

In these spring rolls, chicken is marinated in orange juice, ginger, and soy and then sautéed and combined with crisp apple slices. I prefer using organic chickens raised on a hormone- and antibiotic-free diet. Serve these spring rolls along with a salad or soup for lunch. They also make a crowd-pleasing party appetizer.

MAKES 12 SPRING ROLLS

1 small fresh red chile pepper, minced

3 garlic cloves, minced

2 teaspoons minced fresh ginger

3 tablespoons fresh orange juice

1 tablespoon soy sauce

1 tablespoon rice wine or dry sherry

½ pound boneless, skinless chicken breast, thinly sliced into strips

1 tablespoon extra-virgin olive oil

1 large tart apple, peeled, cored, and cut into thin strips

4 green onions, green part only, cut into short, thin slivers

1 small red bell pepper, seeded and cut into thin strips

1 tablespoon seasoned rice vinegar

1½ teaspoons sesame oil

Twelve 8-inch round dried rice paper wrappers (see page 12)

1 head Boston or Bibb lettuce, leaves washed and separated

Spicy Honey-Basil Sauce (page 36), for serving

1. Combine the chile, garlic, ginger, orange juice, soy sauce, and rice wine in a medium bowl. Add the chicken strips and toss to coat. Cover and marinate in the refrigerator for 15 minutes. Drain excess liquid.

2. In a small nonstick skillet over medium-high heat, heat the olive oil. Add the chicken and sauté until lightly browned and no longer pink, about 2 minutes.

3. Combine the apple, green onions, bell pepper, rice vinegar, and sesame oil in a medium bowl and toss to coat. Stir in the cooked chicken.

4. Fill a medium bowl with warm water. Dip one of the wrappers in the water for 15 seconds, or until softened. Carefully transfer to a dry work surface.

5. Place 2 to 3 tablespoons of the filling in an even horizontal mound just below the center of the wrapper. Roll up the rice paper to form a tight cylinder, folding in the sides about halfway. Assemble the remaining spring rolls in the same manner. Cover the finished rolls with a damp cloth to prevent them from drying out.

6. Preheat the broiler. Lightly coat a large nonstick baking sheet with cooking spray. Arrange the spring rolls on the baking sheet in a single layer, leaving a little space between them. Lightly coat the rolls with cooking spray.

7. Broil the rolls until lightly browned and crisp, 10 to 13 minutes. Using tongs or a spatula, turn the rolls over and continue to broil for another 8 to 10 minutes. Serve each roll wrapped in a lettuce leaf accompanied by the Spicy Honey-Basil Sauce.

mango-lobster spring rolls

Use fresh lobster if it is available. Once cooked, the lobster is wrapped in rice paper with sweet mango and served with Green Tea–Orange Sauce. Fresh crabmeat or shrimp are delicious alternatives.

Refreshing, light, and exotic, these spring rolls make a perfect appetizer for a summer party. Just be sure your guests save room to enjoy the main course.

MAKES 12 SPRING ROLLS

2 tablespoons fish sauce

1 tablespoon rice wine or dry sherry

3½ teaspoons minced fresh ginger

1 tablespoon chopped fresh cilantro leaves

½ pound cooked lobster meat, broken into chunks

2 tablespoons extra-virgin olive oil

1 tablespoon loose green tea, such as gunpowder

2 small mangoes, peeled, pitted, and diced

Twelve 8-inch round dried rice paper wrappers (see page 12)

½ cup Green Tea–Orange Sauce (page 30), for serving

1. Combine the fish sauce, rice wine, 1½ teaspoons of the ginger, and the cilantro in a medium bowl. Add the lobster meat and toss to combine. Cover and marinate in the refrigerator for 30 minutes.

2. Heat the oil in a wok or nonstick skillet over medium-high heat and swirl to coat. Add the green tea and sauté until fragrant, about 30 seconds. Add the remaining 2 teaspoons ginger and sauté for another 30 seconds. Add the lobster mixture and stir and toss until it is heated through, about 1 minute. Remove from the heat and set aside to cool. Once the mixture is cool, stir in the mangoes.

3. Fill a medium bowl with warm water. Dip one of the wrappers in the water for 15 seconds, or until softened. Carefully transfer to a dry work surface.

4. Arrange 2 to 3 tablespoons of the filling in an even horizontal mound just below the center of the wrapper. Roll up the rice paper to form a tight cylinder, folding in the sides about halfway. Assemble the remaining spring rolls in the same manner. Cover the finished rolls with a damp cloth to prevent them from drying out.

5. Serve the rolls at room temperature with the Green Tea–Orange Sauce.

peach-shrimp spring rolls

When I was young, my mother often made spring rolls for my birthday parties, because it is in early March. To this day, spring rolls remain one of my favorite comfort foods. Now, I enjoy experimenting with different fillings and sauces.

In this recipe, I pair spicy, marinated shrimp with sweet, fresh peaches and pungent basil. The wine, chile pepper, and ginger in these rolls help shake the blustery early-spring chill, while the shrimp stimulates yang and nourishes the kidneys.

MAKES 20 SPRING ROLLS; 2 PER SERVING

marinade

1 tablespoon rice wine or dry sherry

1 tablespoon Thai fish sauce

1½ teaspoons fresh lemon juice

1 small, fresh red chile pepper, such as Fresno, seeded and minced (about 2 tablespoons)

3 garlic cloves, minced

2 teaspoons minced fresh ginger

1 tablespoon chopped fresh cilantro leaves

20 medium shrimp (about 4½ ounces), peeled and deveined

filling

1 peach, peeled, pitted, and diced

4 green onions, green part only, cut into thin slivers

1 small red bell pepper, seeded and diced

1 small yellow bell pepper, seeded and diced

1 tablespoon rice vinegar

1½ teaspoons toasted sesame oil

1 tablespoon extra-virgin olive oil

Twenty 8-inch rice-paper wrappers (see page 12)

20 fresh basil or mint leaves

1 cup Spicy Sesame Sauce (page 37), for serving

1. **TO PREPARE THE MARINADE:** Combine the rice wine, fish sauce, lemon juice, chile, garlic, ginger, and cilantro in a medium bowl. Add the shrimp and toss to mix and coat. Cover and marinate in the refrigerator for 30 minutes.

2. **TO MAKE THE FILLING:** Combine the peach, green onions, bell peppers, vinegar, and sesame oil in a medium bowl and toss to mix and coat.

3. Heat a wok or nonstick skillet over medium-high heat. Add the olive oil and swirl to coat the pan evenly. Add the shrimp and marinade and stir-fry until the shrimp turn pink, 1 to 2 minutes. Remove from the heat and set aside.

4. **TO ASSEMBLE THE SPRING ROLLS:** Fill a medium bowl with warm. Dip one of the wrappers in the water for 15 seconds, or until softened. Carefully transfer to a dry work surface.

5. Center 1 basil leaf in the bottom third of the wrapper. Top with a shrimp and 2 tablespoons of the filling. Roll up the wrapper to form a tight cylinder, folding in the sides about halfway. Assemble the remaining spring rolls in the same manner. Cover the finished rolls with a damp cloth to prevent them from drying out.

6. Serve the rolls at room temperature with the Spicy Sesame Sauce.

avocado and smoked salmon spring rolls

Cooling jicama goes nicely with creamy avocado and flavorful smoked salmon. This is one of the few dishes that I won't enlist my family's help for, as they most likely will snack on the ingredients before they have a chance to be assembled. You can substitute juicy Asian pears for the crunchy and sweet jicama.

MAKES 12 SPRING ROLLS

⅓ cup minced red onion

1 tablespoon low-sodium soy sauce

2 teaspoons extra-virgin olive oil

1 teaspoon cayenne pepper

1 small jicama, peeled and diced (about 1 cup)

8 ounces smoked salmon, thinly sliced

2 medium avocados, pitted, peeled, and diced

Twelve 8-inch round dried rice paper wrappers (see page 12)

Sweet-and-Sour Chile Sauce (page 31), for serving

1. Combine the onion, soy sauce, oil, and cayenne in a medium bowl. Stir in the jicama, salmon, and avocados. Cover and marinate in the refrigerator for 10 minutes.

2. Fill a medium bowl with warm water. Dip one of the wrappers in the water for 15 seconds, or until softened. Carefully transfer to a dry work surface.

3. Arrange 2 to 3 tablespoons of the filling in an even horizontal mound just below the center of the wrapper. Roll up the rice paper to form a tight cylinder, folding in the sides about halfway. Assemble the remaining spring rolls in the same manner. Cover the finished rolls with a damp cloth to prevent them from drying out.

4. Serve the rolls, whole or cut in half, with the Sweet-and-Sour Chile Sauce.

warm asparagus-shiitake spring rolls with wasabi

I was inspired to create this recipe after eating a salad seasoned with wasabi in a restaurant in San Francisco. It convinced me that wasabi is more than a condiment for sushi.

Asparagus and shiitake mushrooms are a meant-for-each-other combination, but other mushrooms and vegetables can be substituted. Maitake mushrooms and cucumbers also pair nicely.

MAKES 8 SPRING ROLLS

1 tablespoon white miso

2 tablespoons warm water

1½ teaspoons rice wine or dry sherry

2 tablespoons walnut or olive oil

2 cups (about 6 ounces) fresh shiitake mushroom caps, thinly sliced

½ pound asparagus spears, woody lower ends trimmed

Eight 8-inch round dried rice paper wrappers (see page 12)

¼ cup wasabi paste

Lime-Soy-Ginger Sauce (page 32), for serving

1. In a small bowl, dissolve the miso in the warm water. Mix in the rice wine. Set aside.

2. Heat the walnut oil in a wok or nonstick skillet over medium-high heat and swirl to coat the pan. Add the mushrooms and sauté until softened, about 2 minutes. Add the asparagus spears and cook, stirring, until heated through, about 1 minute. Stir in the miso mixture. Remove from the heat and set aside to cool.

3. Fill a medium bowl with warm water. Dip one of the wrappers in the water for 15 seconds, or until softened. Carefully transfer to a dry work surface.

4. Spread about 1 teaspoon of the wasabi paste horizontally just below the center of the wrapper. Top the wasabi with 2 tablespoons of the spring roll filling in an even horizontal mound. Roll up the rice paper to form a tight cylinder, folding in the sides about halfway. Assemble the remaining spring rolls in the same manner. Cover the finished rolls with a damp cloth to prevent them from drying out.

5. Serve the rolls, whole or cut in half, with the Lime-Soy-Ginger Sauce.

whole wheat flour tortillas

Although ready-made tortillas are available on every grocery store shelf, some contain partially hydrogenated vegetable oil (trans-fatty acids) and lack the nutritional benefits of whole wheat flour. Making homemade tortillas is easy, and the results are far more flavorful and healthy. Before he left for college, my son and his friends loved helping me make these tortillas while I prepared the filling. Nothing pleased me more than having a kitchen full of laughing teenagers.

MAKES 8 TORTILLAS

1 cup whole wheat flour

1 cup all-purpose flour

½ teaspoon salt

3 tablespoons extra-virgin olive oil

½ cup water, or more as needed

1. Combine the flours and salt in a large bowl. Sprinkle in the oil and blend thoroughly with a fork. Gradually add ½ cup water, stirring to moisten evenly. If the dough is too dry to gather into a ball, add a bit more water. Turn the dough out onto a lightly floured work surface and knead briefly, 15 to 20 times. The dough should be soft and easy to knead, but not sticky.

2. Divide the dough into 8 equal pieces. Flatten each one between lightly floured palms into a 3-inch disk. Cover with plastic wrap and let rest for 30 minutes.

3. On a lightly floured surface, using a rolling pin, roll out each tortilla into a 7- to 8-inch rough circle. To prevent them from sticking together, place parchment paper or wax paper between each layer. Keep the tortillas covered with a damp towel as you work.

4. Preheat an 8-inch or larger skillet over medium-high heat until hot. Cook each tortilla until it is speckled with brown spots and puffed, about 45 seconds per side.

two easy ways to heat tortillas

Oven: Preheat the oven to 300°F (149°C). Stack the tortillas (about 4 per batch) and wrap tightly in aluminum foil. Place in the oven for 5 to 10 minutes, or until warm.

Microwave: Stack 4 tortillas between damp paper towels and microwave on high for 30 seconds, or until hot and pliable.

curried beef-mango wraps

Warming ginger, jalapeño chiles, and curry give the beef an exhilerating flavor. Once seared, the meat is wrapped in a whole wheat tortilla, stuffed with juicy, sweet mango, and served with the cooling raita. The overall flavor is truly unforgettable. It's a tasty and satisfying choice for any picnic.

MAKES 8 WRAPS

1 slightly underripe mango, peeled, pitted, and cut into matchstick-size strips

1 tablespoon fresh lemon juice

8 Whole Wheat Flour Tortillas (page 118) or store-bought tortillas

1 tablespoon olive oil

½ cup chopped green onions

1 tablespoon minced fresh ginger

1 tablespoon grated orange zest

1 tablespoon finely chopped jalapeño or serrano chile

1 pound precut stir-fry beef or beef sirloin, trimmed and sliced against the grain into ⅛-inch-thick pieces

1 tablespoon rice wine or dry sherry

1 teaspoon curry powder

Salt

Freshly ground black pepper

1½ cups Cucumber Raita (page 43) or low-fat plain yogurt

1. In a medium bowl, toss the mango strips with the lemon juice. Set aside.

2. Heat the tortillas (see "Two Easy Ways to Heat Tortillas," page 119).

3. Heat a wok or nonstick skillet over medium-high heat. Add the oil and tilt the pan to coat it evenly. Add the green onions, ginger, orange zest, and jalapeño. Cook, stirring, until fragrant, about 1 minute.

4. Add the beef and stir-fry for 1 minute. Add the rice wine and curry powder. Cook, stirring, until the beef is no longer pink on the outside, about 1 minute. Season to taste with salt and pepper. Transfer to a medium bowl. Add the mango and toss to combine.

5. Spoon about ½ cup of the beef mixture into each warm tortilla. Top with 2 tablespoons of the raita. Roll up each tortilla and serve with the remaining raita for dipping.

seared steak wraps with mango and snow peas

The first time I ate pork chops and applesauce, the combination intrigued me. The pairing of the sweet sauce with meat was something my Chinese palate had never experienced before. I decided to experiment with my own meat-and-fruit pairings. This hearty wrap with sliced steak and juicy sweet mango is one of my successes.

MAKES 8 WRAPS

1 pound beef flank steak, thinly sliced

2 tablespoons low-sodium soy sauce

1 tablespoon rice wine or dry sherry

2 teaspoons sesame oil

1 green onion, minced

1 tablespoon cornstarch

Eight 10-inch Whole Wheat Flour Tortillas (page 118) or store-bought tortillas

2 tablespoons extra-virgin olive oil

1½ teaspoons loose green tea

2 teaspoons minced fresh ginger

¾ pound snow peas, trimmed and cut into strips

2 small mangoes, peeled, pitted, and cut into strips

1. Combine the steak, soy sauce, rice wine, sesame oil, green onion, and cornstarch in a medium bowl. Cover and marinate in the refrigerator for 30 minutes or overnight.

2. Heat the tortillas (see "Two Easy Ways to Heat Tortillas," page 119).

3. Remove the beef mixture from the refrigerator. Heat the oil in a wok or non-stick skillet over medium-high heat and swirl to coat the pan. Add the green tea and ginger and sauté until fragrant, about 30 seconds. Add the beef mixture and cook, stirring, until the beef is no longer pink on the outside, about 1 minute. Add the snow peas and stir-fry until they brighten in color, about 1 minute. Remove from the heat.

4. Lay each warm tortilla on a work surface. Arrange ½ cup of the meat mixture and ¼ cup of the mangoes in the center of each wrap. Roll up and serve while warm.

lion's head meatballs in lettuce leaves

In many Asian cultures, lions are believed to ward off evil. These meatballs are called "Lion's Head" simply because of their large size. To save time, you can cook the meatballs a day or two ahead, store them, covered, in the refrigerator, and reheat them in the sauce just before serving. Leftover meatballs will soak up the ginger-coconut sauce and be even more flavorful the next day.

MAKES 8 MEATBALLS

ginger-coconut sauce

½ cup unsweetened light coconut milk

½ cup soy milk

2 tablespoons Thai fish sauce

2 tablespoons minced fresh ginger

2 teaspoons minced hot red chile pepper

1 tablespoon chopped green onions

meatballs

1 pound lean ground pork or beef

½ cup chopped green onions

¼ cup minced leeks, white and light green parts only

1 tablespoon finely chopped fresh ginger

2 teaspoons minced hot red chile pepper

2 tablespoons cornstarch

1 tablespoon all-purpose flour

2 tablespoons sesame oil

½ teaspoon salt

¼ teaspoon ground white pepper

7½ teaspoons extra-virgin olive oil

1 medium head iceberg or Boston lettuce

¼ cup chopped fresh basil or Thai basil leaves, for garnish

1 tablespoon grated lemon zest, for garnish

1. **TO PREPARE THE SAUCE:** Combine the coconut milk, soy milk, Thai fish sauce, ginger, chile, and green onions in a small bowl.

2. **TO MAKE THE MEATBALLS:** Place the pork, green onions, leeks, ginger, chile, cornstarch, flour, sesame oil, salt, and white pepper in a large mixing bowl. Mix by hand until the ingredients are thoroughly combined and the mixture

becomes sticky. Divide the mixture into 8 equal portions, about ¼ cup each. Roll each portion into a ball. Set the balls on an oiled plate.

3. Heat the olive oil in a wok or nonstick skillet over medium-high heat, swirling to coat the pan. Add the meatballs and pan-fry, turning occasionally, for 8 to 10 minutes, until browned on all sides. Transfer to paper towels to drain.

4. Boil the sauce in a large saucepan over medium-high heat. Add the meatballs, cover, and reduce the heat to low. Simmer for about 8 minutes, or until cooked through.

5. Arrange the lettuce leaves on a serving platter. Nestle one meatball in each of the leaves. Garnish with the basil and lemon zest and serve warm.

tofu and cashew lettuce cups

Whenever I bring this dish to a party, it always disappears in minutes. It makes a tasty accompaniment to grilled meat or a refreshing appetizer for a dinner buffet. The green apple, water chestnuts, and cashews make for a satisfying crunch, a perfect contrast to the crisp, low-calorie lettuce leaves.

If you are in a hurry and don't have homemade Chile-Garlic Sauce on hand, you can find one in the Asian section of grocery stores. Just be sure to look for a brand that is low in sodium.

MAKES 24 LETTUCE CUPS; 2 PER SERVING

4 medium heads Boston lettuce, leaves washed and separated

sauce

2 teaspoons cornstarch

¾ cup Chile-Garlic Sauce (page 27)

3 garlic cloves, minced

filling

2 tablespoons extra-virgin olive oil

2 teaspoons minced fresh ginger

2 garlic cloves, minced

¼ pound fresh oyster mushrooms, finely chopped

One 8-ounce package flavor-baked tofu (see page 4), cut into ½-inch cubes

½ cup finely diced carrot

½ cup finely diced green apple

½ cup canned water chestnuts, rinsed and finely diced

½ cup unsalted cashews, toasted (see page 99) and coarsely chopped

2 green onions, trimmed and minced

1 teaspoon toasted sesame oil

1. **TO PREPARE THE SAUCE:** Put the cornstarch in a small bowl. Gradually whisk in ¼ cup of the Chile-Garlic Sauce along with the minced garlic. Set aside. Reserve the remaining Chile-Garlic Sauce for serving.

2. **TO MAKE THE FILLING:** Heat a wok or nonstick skillet over medium-high heat. Add the oil and swirl the pan to coat. Add the ginger and garlic and stir-fry until fragrant, about 30 seconds. Add the mushrooms and tofu and stir-fry for 2 minutes. Add the carrot, apple, and water chestnuts and stir-fry for 30 seconds.

3. Add the dipping sauce–cornstarch mixture. Cook, stirring, until the vegetables are heated through and the sauce is thick, about 2 minutes. Add the cashews, green onions, and sesame oil and toss to combine.

4. Spoon about 2 tablespoons of the filling into each lettuce leaf cup and serve with the remaining Chile-Garlic Sauce.

the art of stir-fry

"Have you done your stir-fry?" is a common greeting used by people in my hometown around mealtime. It's a friendly way of asking someone if they've eaten yet.

For centuries, stir-frying has been an important cooking method in China. Fresh vegetables and rice or noodles are always the focus of the dish. Seafood, meat, nuts, and oils are added in small amounts to enhance the color, texture, and taste. This results in dishes that are low in fat and high in flavor.

As a young girl, stir-fry was a big part of my daily life. I loved to help my grandmother in the kitchen. As she finished chopping the ingredients, I would arrange them on a plate. I'd bounce with excitement when the food she tossed into the wok sizzled and popped. Once the noise died down, I quickly ran to fetch my chopsticks, knowing that in no time I would be enjoying her delicious food.

Traditionally, preparing a stir-fried dish requires a lot of chopping, complex seasonings, and a wok. The good news is that stir-frying is easier than ever now that you can buy precut meats and vegetables in supermarkets. By keeping homemade or store-bought sauces on hand, a healthy meal is always only minutes away. This convenience, combined with the quick, energetic pace of stir-frying, makes it a great match for our busy Western lifestyle.

While a wok is useful, a deep, sloped skillet or chef's pan works just as well. Add a spatula and some sauces, and you are on your way to giving cold, raw ingredients a new, delicious life.

The sauces you select give the dishes an infinite variety of personalities, from hot-tempered Turmeric Chicken (page 143) to enlightened Forbidden Rice with Eggs and Almonds (page 140) and satisfying Pad Thai with Tofu and Pine Nuts (page 151). Let your stir-fry's "personality" cater to your mood as individual fresh ingredients quickly meld to take on a new, delicious form.

yin-yang rice balls

During China's Cultural Revolution, when the time came for the "reeducation" of bourgeois children, I had to walk for two hours to a farm to pull weeds all day. When the weather was cold and harsh, my grandmother made me spicy rice balls. The chile peppers in the rice balls kept me warm, the brown rice gave me energy, and the sesame seeds helped keep my blood circulating. Now, in autumn, I always pack these treats when my family goes on hikes.

Recently, I created a sweet white rice ball and found that it makes a nice complement to the spicy rice balls. Make both versions and serve them together as a striking appetizer for a dinner party, or with afternoon tea. You can find both sweet brown rice and white rice in Asian grocery stores or health food stores.

MAKES 6 SERVINGS; 3 RICE BALLS PER SERVING

brown rice mixture

4 cups water

3 black tea bags

1½ cups spinach leaves or other leafy greens

1 tablespoon extra-virgin olive oil

½ cup baked tofu, minced, any flavor

¼ cup carrots, minced

1 teaspoon fresh red chile pepper, minced

2 green onions, green part only, minced

2 cups cooked sweet brown rice

2 tablespoons soy sauce

2 teaspoons sesame oil

1 teaspoon freshly ground black pepper

white rice mixture

2 cups cooked warm sweet white rice

¼ cup dried cherries, minced

¼ cup dried dates, minced

¼ cup dried currants

Honey or maple syrup

1½ cups black sesame seeds, toasted (see page 32)

1½ cups white sesame seeds, toasted (see page 32)

Banana leaves, for lining the plate

(continued)

1. **TO MAKE THE BROWN RICE MIXTURE:** In a small pot, bring the water to a boil. Add the tea bags and spinach leaves. Blanch until the spinach leaves are soft, about 15 seconds; be careful not to overcook. Drain and rinse under cold running water. Squeeze out excess water and mince.

2. Heat the olive oil over medium-high heat in a wok or nonstick skillet. Add the tofu, carrots, and chile and sauté until the tofu browns, about 2 minutes. Add the spinach and green onions and stir-fry for 1 minute. Stir in the brown rice, soy sauce, sesame oil, and black pepper. Mix thoroughly and let the rice heat through. Transfer the mixture to a bowl and set aside to cool slightly.

3. **TO MAKE THE WHITE RICE MIXTURE:** In a large mixing bowl, combine the white rice, dried fruit, and honey to taste.

4. Put the black and white sesame seeds into two separate shallow bowls. Line a serving plate with banana leaves. If you don't have banana leaves, lightly oil the serving plate.

5. With wet hands, tightly pack about ¼ cup of the brown rice mixture into a ball. Roll it in the black sesame seeds until coated. Repeat with the remaining brown rice mixture. In the same manner, form the white rice mixture into balls and roll in the white sesame seeds.

6. Artistically arrange the spicy and sweet rice balls on the serving plate. Serve at room temperature.

stir-fried bok choy with shiitake mushrooms

I was shocked when one of my friends insisted that bok choy is a bland vegetable with no potential. This dish helped change her mind. Shanghai, or baby, bok choy is sweeter and more tender than its larger cousin. Look for baby bok choy in Asian markets, health food stores, and at farmers' markets. The mushrooms in this dish aid digestion and also act as an anti-inflammatory agent.

While many restaurants use chicken broth to make this Cantonese classic, in my version I substitute green tea and rice milk, making it suitable for vegetarians.

MAKES 4 SERVINGS

3 dried shiitake mushrooms

2 tablespoons extra-virgin olive oil

1½ teaspoons loose green tea

2 garlic cloves, minced

1 pound baby bok choy or regular bok choy, cut into 3-inch pieces

2 tablespoons rice milk or soy milk

1½ teaspoons rice wine or dry sherry

Salt

Freshly ground black pepper

1. Soak the mushrooms in warm water until they soften, about 15 minutes.

2. Rinse the mushrooms under running water. Using your hands, squeeze out any excess water. Cut the mushrooms into 2-inch chunks.

3. Heat a wok or nonstick skillet over medium-high heat. Add the oil and swirl the pan to coat. Add the tea and stir-fry until fragrant, about 30 seconds. Add the garlic and mushrooms and stir-fry until fragrant, about 1 minute.

4. Add the bok choy and immediately cover the pan to prevent the oil from splattering. Give the pan two good shakes and continue cooking for 30 seconds. Remove the lid and stir-fry until the bok choy leaves turn bright green and soften.

5. Add the rice milk and rice wine and stir-fry for 1 minute. Season to taste with salt and pepper. Serve hot.

spicy spinach with sesame seeds

In Asia, amino acid–rich black sesame seeds are believed to keep hair shiny and prevent graying. When I was in China, for years I used shampoos containing black sesame extracts. These days, I just incorporate sesame into many of my dishes.

Spinach is an excellent source of vitamins C and A, and is available throughout the year. The cooling green tea and spinach make this dish a perfect complement to hearty meat dishes.

MAKES 4 SERVINGS

4½ teaspoons extra-virgin olive oil

2 teaspoons loose green tea

3 garlic cloves, minced

1 teaspoon seeded and chopped fresh red chile pepper

1 pound baby spinach

1 tablespoon rice vinegar

Salt

Freshly ground black pepper

2 tablespoons white sesame seeds, toasted (see page 150), for garnish

Cooked rice, for serving

1. Heat a wok or nonstick skillet over medium-high heat. Add the oil and swirl to coat. Add the tea and sauté until fragrant, about 30 seconds. Add the garlic and chile and stir-fry for 30 seconds.

2. Add the spinach and stir-fry for 2 minutes. Stir in the rice vinegar and continue stir-frying until the leaves are slightly wilted, about 1 minute. Season to taste with salt and pepper. Garnish with the sesame seeds and serve hot with the rice.

happy family

There's a dish in China called "Happy Family," which consists of various ingredients. Growing up, my mother's version of "Happy Family" was stir-fried colorful, seasonal fresh vegetables. She would encourage my brothers and me to eat more of it so we would be in harmony.

Fresh vegetables are quickly stir-fried to retain their snap and color for a vibrant presentation. Pair this with Garlic-Pecan Chicken (page 141) or Almond Trout with Mango-Ginger Salsa (page 175). Any leftovers can be served with warm pasta.

MAKES 4 SERVINGS

3 tablespoons extra-virgin olive oil

3 garlic cloves, minced

1 fresh red chile pepper, minced

1½ cups peeled and julienned turnips

1 medium carrot, peeled and julienned

1 small yellow bell pepper, julienned

2 tablespoons low-sodium soy sauce

4½ teaspoons rice wine or dry sherry

1 teaspoon chile sesame oil, for garnish

1. Heat a wok or nonstick skillet over medium-high heat. Add the olive oil and swirl the pan to coat.

2. Add the garlic and chile and sauté until fragrant, about 1 minute. Add the turnips and stir-fry until tender, about 3 minutes. Add the carrot and cook for 1 minute. Add the bell pepper and cook and toss until tender, about 1 minute. Stir in the soy sauce and rice wine. Cook, stirring, until the vegetables are coated. Garnish with the sesame oil. Serve hot.

shredded potatoes with garlic and ginseng

During the wintertime, fresh vegetables used to be hard to come by in the northern region of China. Because potatoes are easy to grow and store, they became the main staple there. TCM uses potatoes to relieve digestive illness caused by excessive stomach acid. They are also a good source of vitamin C and the vitamin B complex.

Traditionally, potatoes are stir-fried with soy sauce and vinegar. I modified this recipe with olive oil, fresh garlic, chile, and chives to make it more exhilarating.

MAKES 4 SERVINGS

1 pound red potatoes, peeled and shredded (see page 20)

3 tablespoons extra-virgin olive oil

3 garlic cloves, minced

½ fresh red chile pepper

Contents of 2 ginseng tea bags

½ cup finely chopped red onion

2 tablespoons rice vinegar

Salt

Ground white pepper

2 tablespoons chopped fresh chives, for garnish

1. Soak the potatoes in cold water for 10 minutes; drain and dry thoroughly.

2. Heat a wok or nonstick skillet over medium-high heat. Add the oil and swirl the pan to coat. Add the garlic, chile, and ginseng and sauté until fragrant, about 1 minute.

3. Add the potatoes and stir-fry until the potatoes are crispy, 3 to 5 minutes. Add the onion and stir-fry until the onion starts to soften, about 2 minutes. Add the rice vinegar and season to taste with salt and white pepper.

4. Transfer to a serving platter and garnish with the chives. Serve hot.

Sautéed Tofu with Edamame and Cranberries (top; page 138)
and Sautéed Kale with Cashes and Raisins (bottom)

sautéed kale with cashews and raisins

Chinese medicine doctors believe that bitter foods, such as kale, maintain emotional balance and improve the appetite. To even out the raw kale's bitter taste, I sauté it with rice milk and sweet raisins. The dried chiles in the dish should not be eaten. They're just meant to add flavor and color.

MAKES 4 SERVINGS

¾ pound kale

2 tablespoons extra-virgin olive oil

1 teaspoon mustard seeds

1 teaspoon cumin seeds

2 dried red chile peppers

¼ cup rice milk

¼ cup golden raisins

Sea salt

¼ cup chopped toasted cashew nuts (see page 99), for garnish

1. Wash the kale thoroughly and drain well. Strip the leaves from the coarse stems and discard the stems. Cut the leaves into 4-inch lengths.

2. Heat a wok or nonstick skillet over medium high heat. Add the oil and swirl the pan to coat. Add the mustard seeds, cumin seeds, and chiles and sauté until fragrant, about 1 minute.

3. Add the kale and cook, stirring, for 1 minute. Add the rice milk and raisins. Cover and cook for 2 minutes. Remove the lid and continue to cook until the kale softens. Season to taste with sea salt. Garnish with the chopped cashews. Serve warm with whole wheat pita bread.

sautéed tofu with edamame and cranberries

During one of my cruise lectures, I was surprised when a guest told me that when she was a child the soybean was used primarily as cattle feed. When I was young, along with millions of other Chinese, I thrived on soy-based foods, because meat was strictly rationed.

Chinese medicine doctors consider soy yin, or cooling. They prescribe it to treat fevers, headaches, chest distention, and hyperactivity, and as a tonic for the lungs and stomach. Fresh or dried cranberries are a good source of ellagic acid, an antioxidant compound. This is a perfect dish to welcome the spring.

MAKES 4 SERVINGS

1 tablespoon olive oil

8 ounces flavor-baked tofu (see page 4), cut into 1-inch cubes

2 cups shelled frozen edamame (soybeans)

1 cup thinly sliced leeks, white part only

½ cup dried cranberries

1 tablespoon soy sauce

1 tablespoon rice vinegar

2 teaspoons sesame oil

¼ cup pine nuts, toasted (see page 99), for garnish

1. Heat a wok or nonstick skillet over medium-high heat. Add the olive oil and swirl the pan to coat.

2. Add the tofu and stir-fry until golden-brown, about 2 minutes. Add the edamame and stir-fry for 2 minutes, or until heated through. Add the leeks, cranberries, soy sauce, and rice vinegar and stir-fry until heated through, 1 to 2 minutes.

3. Transfer the tofu to a serving dish and drizzle with the sesame oil. Garnish with the toasted pine nuts and serve hot.

buddha's delight

On my last trip to China, I spent a night with a girlfriend at a famous Buddhist temple in southeast China. I was intrigued by the nuns' simple lifestyle. This recipe is inspired by the dish I shared with them.

"Buddha's Delight" is traditionally a mix of vegetarian and soy-based products stir-fried together. Yet this dish will delight your guests, vegetarian or not!

MAKES 4 SERVINGS

One 2.5-ounce package bean thread noodles

1 tablespoon extra-virgin olive oil

3 garlic cloves, minced

1 teaspoon minced fresh ginger

2 ounces fresh oyster mushrooms, coarsely chopped

Contents of 2 ginseng tea bags (optional)

4 ounces flavor-baked tofu (see page 4), cut into 1-inch cubes

2 cups 1-inch pieces Napa cabbage

½ cup shredded bamboo shoots

½ cup Ginger Tea Sauce (page 29)

Salt

Ground white pepper

2 teaspoons sesame oil

3 sprigs fresh cilantro, cut into 2-inch pieces, for garnish

1. Soak the noodles in hot water until soft, about 10 minutes. Drain and set aside.

2. Heat a wok or nonstick skillet over medium-high heat. Add the olive oil and swirl the pan to coat. Add the garlic, ginger, mushrooms, and ginseng and sauté until fragrant, about 1 minute.

3. Add the tofu, cabbage, and bamboo shoots and stir-fry for 2 minutes. Add the noodles and sauce and bring to a boil. Reduce the heat to medium-low, cover, and simmer until the vegetables are tender, about 3 minutes. Season to taste with salt and pepper.

4. Transfer to a serving bowl. Stir in the sesame oil and garnish with the cilantro.

garlic-pecan chicken

Spaniards introduced pecans, native to North America, to Asia in the sixteenth century. Because of their rich, buttery flavor, they were quickly included in many savory Asian dishes and desserts.

TCM believes pecans are neutral in nature. They are often used in remedies to reduce yang, or heat. This amazing nut is a good source of protein and unsaturated fats and contains antioxidants and plant sterols, which reduce high cholesterol.

To save time, use precut chicken breasts. Vary the vegetables based on the season. Serve this dish with steamed brown rice to make a hearty meal.

MAKES 4 SERVINGS

spicy garlic marinade

3 large garlic cloves, minced

¼ teaspoon crushed red pepper flakes, or more as desired

1 tablespoon olive oil

1 tablespoon fresh lemon juice

1 teaspoon salt

chicken

¾ pound chicken breast, cut into thin strips for stir-frying

3 tablespoons extra-virgin olive oil

2 medium bell peppers, any color, seeded and julienned

1 small white onion, halved longthwise and thinly sliced

1 teaspoon salt

¼ teaspoon crushed red pepper flakes, or more as desired

½ cup candied pecans (see page 88), for garnish

1. **TO MAKE THE MARINADE:** Combine the marinade ingredients in a large bowl. Add the chicken and toss to coat. Cover and refrigerate for up to 30 minutes.

2. **TO PREPARE THE CHICKEN:** Heat a wok or nonstick skillet over high heat and coat with 2 tablespoons of the oil. Add the chicken, and reserve the marinade.

(continued)

3. Sauté the chicken until browned and no longer pink in the center, about 2 minutes. Transfer to a bowl.

4. Recoat the wok with the remaining 1 tablespoon oil. Add the bell peppers, onion, salt, red pepper flakes, and reserved marinade. Sauté until the bell peppers soften, about 1 minute.

5. Return the chicken to the wok, stir, and cook until heated through. Garnish with the candied pecans. Serve hot.

turmeric chicken

This dish marries the North African flavors of turmeric, cinnamon, and cumin with the Asian cooking method of stir-frying. Turmeric is a powerful disease-fighting agent and is praised for its anti-inflammatory effect. It is also believed to stimulate the immune system, making this an ideal dish for flu season.

For the best results, marinate the chicken overnight to infuse the meat with flavor. Substitute golden raisins for the dates, if you prefer. Serve with couscous or brown rice.

MAKES 4 SERVINGS

2 teaspoons ground cinnamon

1 tablespoon ground turmeric

½ teaspoon ground cumin

½ teaspoon salt

¼ teaspoon chile powder

4 boneless, skinless chicken breast halves

2 tablespoons extra-virgin olive oil

2 medium Granny Smith apples, peeled, cored, and chopped into small cubes

½ cup whole dates, pitted and sliced

1. Combine 1 teaspoon of the cinnamon with the turmeric, cumin, salt, and chile powder in a resealable plastic bag. Add the chicken and toss well to coat.

2. Heat the oil in a wok or nonstick skillet over medium-high heat. Add the chicken, reduce the heat to medium, and sauté until no longer pink in the center, about 5 minutes per side. Transfer the chicken to a serving platter and cover to keep warm.

3. Sauté the apples and dates in the same wok for 1 minute. Sprinkle with the remaining 1 teaspoon cinnamon and stir to coat.

4. Spoon the apples and dates over the chicken. Serve warm.

turmeric scallops with turnips and cashews

During one of my cruise lectures to Southeast Asia, I was asked on short notice to host a dinner party for the suite guests. When the hotel manager requested that I develop a unique recipe for the event, I came up with this. Everyone loved it, especially after I shared with them the many health benefits of the ingredients.

Scallops are another seafood rich in omega-3 fatty acids, and a good source of magnesium and potassium. Cashews are rich in copper, magnesium, and calcium, and turnips are high in dietary fiber and potassium. Use tender small baby turnips, as they are the tastiest.

MAKES 4 SERVINGS

½ cup Miso-Sesame Sauce (page 33)

2 teaspoons cornstarch

1 pound large scallops

3 tablespoons olive oil

1 tablespoon fresh turmeric, thinly shredded

1½ cups ¼-inch dice turnips

Salt

Freshly ground black pepper

¼ cup toasted cashews (see page 99), for garnish

2 tablespoons chopped fresh flat-leaf parsley, for garnish

1. In a medium bowl, whisk the sauce and cornstarch together. Add the scallops and stir gently to coat. Let marinate for about 3 minutes per side. Gently remove the scallops, and reserve the marinade.

2. Heat 2 tablespoons of the oil in a large skillet over medium-high heat. Add the turmeric and cook, stirring constantly, until fragrant, about 20 seconds. Place the scallops in a single layer and pan-fry until golden brown, about 3 minutes per side. Transfer to a serving plate and cover to keep warm.

3. Heat the remaining 1 tablespoon oil in the skillet. Add the turnips and sauté for 1 minute, then add the reserved cornstarch-sauce mixture. Cook, stirring, until heated through, about 1 minute. Season to taste with salt and pepper.

4. Arrange the turnip mixture around the scallops artistically. Garnish with the cashews and parsley. Serve warm.

emperor's shrimp

The recipe is named "Emperor's Shrimp" because in China it was traditionally cooked with giant tiger prawns, which were rare and exotic, and
reserved for the emperor. I like to use flavorful medium, wild shrimp, as they
are easier to find. To save time, use fresh or frozen shrimp from the store
that are already shelled and deveined.

Walnuts have more omega-3 fatty acids, essential for healthy skin, than
any other nut. In this dish, just a small amount is enough to add a delightful,
sweet crunch that pairs wonderfully with the tender shrimp.

MAKES 4 SERVINGS

marinade
¼ cup Spicy Sesame Sauce (page 37)

4 teaspoons cornstarch

shrimp
1 pound medium raw shrimp, peeled and
deveined

¼ cup olive oil

1 tablespoon loose black tea

3 green onions, julienned

1 medium red bell pepper, seeded and
julienned

¼ cup canned walnuts

Cooked rice or noodles, for serving

1. **TO MAKE THE MARINADE:** Combine the sauce and the cornstarch in a medium
   bowl. Add the shrimp and toss to coat. Cover and refrigerate for 30 minutes.

2. **TO PREPARE THE SHRIMP:** In a wok or nonstick skillet heat 2 tablespoons of
   the oil and swirl to coat. Add the tea and sauté over medium-high heat until
   fragrant, about 30 seconds. Add the shrimp and cook, stirring, until it turns
   pink, about 1 minute. Transfer to a bowl.

3. Recoat the wok with the remaining 2 tablespoons oil. Add the green onions
   and bell pepper and sauté for 1 minute. Return the shrimp to the wok, stir, and
   cook until heated through. Toss in the walnuts. Serve with rice or noodles.

brown rice stir-fry with flavored tofu and vegetables

Although white rice is traditional in Asian cooking, I prefer brown rice because it contains more fiber and nutrients, such as B vitamins and phosphorus, than its lighter counterpart. Sweet brown rice has a mild flavor. You can find it in most health food stores or gourmet food shops, or, in a pinch, substitute regular long-grain brown rice.

MAKES 4 SERVINGS

2 tablespoons extra-virgin olive oil

3 garlic cloves, minced

One 3-inch piece fresh ginger, chopped

8 ounces flavor-baked tofu (see page 4), cut into 1-inch cubes

1 medium red bell pepper, seeded and cut into 1-inch pieces

1 medium yellow bell pepper, seeded and cut into 1-inch pieces

3 cups cooked sweet brown rice or long-grain brown rice

3 tablespoons reduced-sodium soy sauce

1 teaspoon toasted sesame oil

Salt

Freshly ground black pepper

3 green onions, halved lengthwise and thinly sliced, for garnish

1. In a large wok or nonstick skillet, heat the olive oil over medium-high heat. Add the garlic and ginger and stir-fry until fragrant, about 30 seconds.

2. Add the tofu and stir-fry until golden brown, about 2 minutes. Add the bell peppers and cook, stirring, until they are crisp-tender, about 3 minutes.

3. Add the rice and soy sauce and cook, stirring occasionally, until the rice is heated through, about 3 minutes. Stir in the sesame oil. Season to taste with salt and pepper. Divide equally among four plates and garnish with the green onions. Serve hot.

forbidden rice with eggs and almonds

Forbidden rice, also known as black rice, was once cultivated solely for the emperors of China, but now you can find it in Asian markets and health food stores. Like brown rice, forbidden rice requires a little more water and time to cook than white rice.

According to TCM, black rice replenishes the blood. Eggs combat colds and infections. Shiitake mushrooms and almonds strengthen the immune system. Together, they make an ideal comfort food for brisk fall weather, and for those suffering from stomach chills and weak digestion. The black rice, red cranberries, and colorful vegetables make for a pleasing contrast that will cheer your spirits and brighten your table.

MAKES 4 SERVINGS

2 large organic eggs, lightly beaten

1½ teaspoons soy sauce, plus more as needed

2 teaspoons sesame oil

1 green onion, sliced

1 tablespoon olive oil

¼ pound ham, cut into ½-inch cubes

¼ cup fresh shiitake mushrooms, stemmed,

caps cut into 1-inch-wide strips

¼ cup green peas, fresh or frozen

1½ cups cooked black or brown rice

2 green onions, white part only, sliced, for garnish

¼ cup toasted, crushed almonds (see page 99), for garnish

¼ cup dried cranberries, for garnish

1. In a bowl, beat together the eggs, soy sauce, and sesame oil until well blended. Stir in the green onion and set aside.

2. Heat the olive oil in a nonstick sauté pan over medium-high heat and swirl to coat. Pour in the egg mixture. Cook, without stirring, until the egg is softly set. Break up the egg with a spatula. Add the ham, shiitake mushrooms, peas, and cooked rice. Cook, stirring, until the rice mixture is heated through. Season with additional soy sauce to taste. Garnish with the sliced green onions, almonds, and cranberries. Serve hot.

harmony holiday delight

Food is highly symbolic in Chinese culture, with dishes to represent nearly every aspect of people's aspirations, such as long noodles for a long, happy life, dumplings for togetherness, and fish for abundance. Just like "Happy Family," this colorful and wholesome dish, often served during Chinese New Year's gatherings, is emblematic of the harmony that exists between friends and family members.

MAKES 6 SERVINGS

3 tablespoons extra-virgin olive oil

5 garlic cloves, minced

4½ teaspoons minced fresh ginger

1 fresh red chile pepper, minced

¼ pound fresh shiitake mushroom caps, cut into ½-inch cubes

2 cups shelled fresh or frozen edamame (soybeans)

1 cup frozen sweet baby corn

½ cup soy milk

1 tablespoon rice vinegar

1 cup dried cherries or cranberries

Salt

Ground white pepper

1 hothouse cucumber, thinly sliced

3 plum tomatoes, thinly sliced

2 tablespoons black sesame seeds, toasted (see page 32), for garnish

1. Heat a wok or nonstick skillet over medium-high heat. Add the oil and swirl the pan to coat. Add the garlic, ginger, chile, and mushrooms and stir-fry until fragrant, 1 to 2 minutes.

2. Add the edamame and stir-fry for 1 minute. Mix in the corn, soy milk, and rice vinegar and cook, stirring, until most of the liquid evaporates, 2 to 3 minutes.

3. Mix in the cherries. Season to taste with the salt and white pepper.

4. Arrange the cucumber and tomato slices in an alternating pattern around the perimeter of a serving plate. Pile the cooked vegetables in the center. Garnish with the toasted sesame seeds and serve immediately.

pad thai with tofu and pine nuts

Long before I visited Bangkok and Chiang Mai, I was enraptured with Thai cuisine, especially the sauces they use for their noodle dishes. I find that many restaurants use a chicken-based sauce. In this dish, I substitute tofu for the traditional eggs and use a lime-peanut sauce to make it vegan friendly. Double or triple the recipe when you can; this is one of those dishes that taste even better the next day.

MAKES 4 SERVINGS

8 ounces dry rice noodles

3 tablespoons extra-virgin olive oil

1 cup fresh shiitake mushrooms, stemmed, caps cut into 1-inch-wide strips

8 ounces flavor-baked tofu (see page 4), julienned

½ cup julienned red bell pepper

2 cups sunflower sprouts or daikon radish sprouts, rinsed and drained

1 cup Lime-Peanut Sauce (page 35)

¼ cup fresh mint leaves, for garnish

3 tablespoons toasted pine nuts (see page 99), for garnish

1. Cook the rice noodles according to package directions. Drain and rinse with cold water to prevent sticking. Set aside.

2. Heat the oil in a wok or nonstick skillet. Add the mushrooms and tofu and cook, stirring gently, until the tofu browns, about 2 minutes.

3. Add the bell pepper and cook for 1 minute. Add the sprouts and stir-fry for 30 seconds. Stir in the noodles and sauce and combine thoroughly. Transfer to a serving dish. Garnish with the mint and pine nuts. Serve warm or cold.

pan-fried udon noodles

Use the best-quality green tea you can find for this dish. One excellent choice is gunpowder, so called because the tea looks like little balls of black gunpowder. As you sauté, the tea will unfurl and release an intoxicating aroma.

Seaweed is a nutritious sea vegetable rich in iron and iodine that is believed to nourish and stimulate the digestive system. It comes in sheets, threads, strips, and granules. Some types are dry and must be soaked in warm water to soften before cooking. Other varieties have been roasted and require no cooking. Roasted seaweed can be added directly to dishes.

MAKES 4 SERVINGS

9 ounces fresh or dried udon noodles

2 tablespoons extra-virgin olive oil

2 teaspoons loose green tea, preferably gunpowder

2 garlic cloves, finely chopped

1½ teaspoons minced fresh ginger

4 ounces flavor baked tofu (see page 4), cut into 1-inch cubes

1 medium carrot, cut into matchstick-size strips

1 medium daikon, cut into matchstick-size strips

1 medium leek, white part only, cut into long matchstick-size strips

3 tablespoons Green Tea–Orange Sauce (page 30)

1 tablespoon rice vinegar

¼ cup roasted seaweed or toasted black sesame seeds (see page 32), for garnish

1. Cook the noodles according to the package directions. Drain and rinse under cold water. Set aside.

2. Heat a wok or nonstick skillet over medium-high heat. Add the oil and swirl the pan to coat. Add the tea and stir-fry until fragrant, about 30 seconds. Add the garlic, ginger, and tofu and stir-fry until the tofu is golden brown, about 2 minutes. Add the carrot, daikon, and leek and stir-fry for 1 minute.

3. Mix in the noodles, sauce, and rice vinegar. Cook, stirring occasionally, until the noodles are heated through. Garnish with the roasted seaweed or sesame seeds. Serve hot or cold.

outdoor
cooking
grilled food

In China, like many families there, we cooked all of our food on a small coal stove, and later, a gas stove. The first time I tasted grilled food was at a barbecue party put on by my graduate school advisor at the University of Colorado, Boulder.

I was astonished when she brought out a tray laden with precut fish, meat and vegetables still in their packages, and delegated control of the grill to two of my classmates who had volunteered. While they cooked the food, she sat in one of the lawn chairs and enjoyed the conversation with us. Everything seemed so simple and hassle free. I couldn't help remembering the parties my mother hosted. She could never take a break from washing, cutting, and cooking in the kitchen, let alone have a chance to sit down and enjoy a long conversation with guests.

Even though I disliked the hot dogs and the thick steaks served at the party, I enjoyed the fish and vegetables, and most importantly, the casual, relaxed atmosphere and great conversation. It reminded me of my times spent with friends and family in China.

During my next monthly phone call with my mother, I excitedly described the party to her. She listened quietly as I described the barbecue. In her next letter, she voiced her concern over my diet, and stressed that grilled foods, especially meats, are laden with heat, and that if I consumed them in the summer, I should balance the excess yang with yin foods. Since then, I always serve a cooling salad or salsa alongside grilled foods, and marinate the meats in a complementary sauce. Many of the sauces in this book can be used as a delicious marinade. They contain less fat and sodium than most commercial brands and are high in healthful components.

COOKING WITH AN ASIAN ACCENT

Studies have shown that foods do not absorb the marinade once they are on the grill. So for optimal flavor, allow time to marinate before cooking, as directed in the recipes. Besides infusing the meat with flavor, marinating prevents the rapid loss of water from its surface during grilling, which can cause harmful heterocyclic amine mutagens to form. It's an important sanitary practice to stop basting a few minutes before the end of cooking and discard any unused marinade.

By following the simple recipes in this chapter, even the most timid take-out chef should be able to confidently prepare a delicious meal. Or, you can follow the example of my advisor, and enjoy the party while letting your guests cook for you!

general guides to grilling

- Clean the grill with a stiff wire brush before grilling.

- Before lighting the grill, spray the rack with a nonstick cooking spray, or brush it lightly with oil to prevent food from sticking to the rack.

- Marinate meats and season vegetables before grilling. If your marinade contains sugar or alcohol, use a lower heat, as your food will burn if the temperature is too high or if it is exposed to heat for too long.

- Use high temperatures for quick-cooking cuts, such as boneless, skinless chicken breasts, shrimp, and fish fillets. Use low heat for slower-cooking cuts, such as ribs and thick steaks.

- Avoid cooking the food at high temperatures for a prolonged time, because this is when carcinogens form.

- Keep the grill lid closed while grilling so the grill works more like an oven and cooks food more evenly. The food will also cook faster and use less fuel. Most important, the cover cuts off some of the oxygen, making it less likely that you will get flare-ups.

- Turn vegetables and fruit frequently during grilling for even cooking.

- Use nonstick fish holders or a nonstick tray for cooking whole fish or fish fillets on the grill.

- For best results, turn fish only once during grilling.

- Always wear oven mitts when handling hot food.

testing for doneness

Unlike other cooking methods, times for grilled food vary due to many factors that affect the cooking process. This includes the type of the grill and the source of the heat, how clean and airtight your grill is, what other foods you are grilling at the same time, how often you peek, and even how windy it is in your backyard. There are also the considerations of temperature, the freshness of your food, the type of marinade you are using, and individual preference for doneness.

So, let your nose and eyes, not the clock, help determine when the food is done to your liking. Use the cooking times in the recipes and the following guidelines to determine doneness.

meat. Make a small cut into the thickest part. It should no longer show pink inside for poultry. Beef should be cooked to each individual's preference. For a large cut, use an instant-read thermometer to check if the cut has reached a safe internal temperature of 150° to 170°F (68° to 76°C) for most meats and chicken.

fish. Test the interior of the fish with a fork; it should just begin to flake. The outside of the fish should be crispy.

shrimp and scallops. Shrimp and scallops should lose their translucence and become opaque throughout.

vegetables and fruit. These should be light golden brown on the outside and tender inside.

grilled shiitake mushrooms

Shiitake mushrooms are a common ingredient in Asian dishes. They are believed to have antiviral, immune-system-strengthening, and antitumor effects. As a child, most of the shiitakes I ate were dried because fresh ones were rare. When I first saw large, fresh, organic shiitake mushrooms, I could hardly contain my excitement. Mushrooms are perfect for the grill. As they release their moisture, their flavor intensifies.

Purchase mushrooms with large caps for this dish. If fresh shiitakes aren't available, portobello mushrooms are a delicious swap. Serve as a side dish or as a sandwich filling along with other grilled vegetables.

MAKES 4 SERVINGS

½ cup extra-virgin olive oil, plus more as needed for brushing the grill

2 garlic cloves, minced

2 green onions, white part only, minced

Salt

Freshly ground black pepper

1 pound large, fresh shiitake mushrooms, stemmed

1. Combine the oil, garlic, green onions, salt, and pepper in a bowl.

2. Add the mushrooms to the marinade. Cover and refrigerate for 4 hours.

3. Brush the grill rack generously with oil and preheat the grill to medium-low. Grill the mushroom caps, brushing with the marinade occasionally, until lightly browned on both sides, about 5 minutes per side. Serve hot.

grilled summer squash and cherry tomatoes

I'm not an experienced gardener, but growing my own vegetables always makes me feel like a seasoned farmer. At the beginning of each summer, I plant a few squash and tomatoes in my garden. The endless harvest of both through the season adds a delightfully fresh splash of taste and color to my meals.

For this recipe, use a grill basket that is designed to be placed directly on the grill to keep small slices of vegetables from slipping into the coals. If you don't have one, line the grill with a large sheet of heavy-duty aluminum foil.

MAKES 6 SERVINGS

1 medium zucchini, cut on the diagonal into 1-inch-thick slices

1 medium yellow squash, cut on the diagonal into 1-inch-thick slices

½ pound cherry tomatoes

3 garlic cloves, minced

1 fresh red chile pepper, chopped

Contents of 3 ginseng tea bags

3 tablespoons Savory Green Tea Oil (page 42) or extra-virgin olive oil, plus more olive oil as needed for brushing the grill

1 tablespoon red vinegar

Salt

Ground white pepper

1. Place all of the ingredients in a bowl and toss to coat. Cover and marinate in the refrigerator for 2 hours.

2. Brush the grill rack generously with oil and preheat the grill to medium. Place the vegetable mixture in a grilling tray. Discard the marinade.

3. Grill the vegetables, turning occasionally, until golden and tender, 4 to 6 minutes. Serve hot.

tofu-vegetable kebabs with curry-peanut sauce

A few years ago, I went to Hanoi, Vietnam. While my fellow travelers visited historical sites, I spent a day wandering around the narrow streets and observed the food peddlers. This dish was inspired by my lunch—seafood and tropical fruit kebabs served with peanut sauce. I created this simple, homemade version by using baked tofu and substituted vegetables for the fruit.

MAKES 4 SERVINGS

Olive oil, as needed for coating the baking pan and brushing the grill

One 16-ounce package extra-firm tofu, drained

1½ cups Curry-Peanut Sauce (page 34)

1 red bell pepper, seeded and cut into 1-inch squares

1 green bell pepper, seeded and cut into 1-inch squares

2 white onions, quartered

1. Preheat the oven to 400°F. Lightly coat a baking pan with oil. Place the tofu on the pan and bake for 30 minutes. Cut the tofu horizontally into 2 large pieces, then cut those in half vertically, and then into quarters to make 8 equal cubes.

2. In a large bowl, combine the tofu, sauce, bell peppers, and onions. Cover and marinate in the refrigerator for 2 hours, turning gently two times. Soak eight 10-inch bamboo skewers in cold water for at least 30 minutes.

3. Oil the grill rack and preheat the grill to medium. Thread alternating pieces of tofu, bell pepper, and onion on the skewers. Place the kebabs on the grill and cook until the kebabs are brown and crisp, 3 to 4 minutes per side.

all about kebabs

THERE ARE TWO TYPES OF SKEWERS to use for grilling kebabs: bamboo or metal. Each has pros and cons. Bamboo skewers are safer and easier to handle hot off the grill than metal ones, especially for children. They also are disposable. However, they must be soaked in cold water for 30 minutes before grilling to prevent them from burning. Even so, their exposed handles are still vulnerable to flame. Remember to place the uncovered handles away from the fire. Or if your grill is small enough, leave the ends of the skewers outside of the heated areas. If you have a larger grill and your kebab requires an extended cooking time, bamboo skewers may not be a good choice. Look for the flat type of metal skewers, which prevents the food from slipping as you turn them during cooking. Metal skewers are good for larger pieces of food and extended cooking times. Their longer size enables you to grill more food at the same time.

Cut foods for kebabs into uniform pieces. Group together those foods that require similar cooking times. Avoid pairing large hunks of meat or hard vegetables with quick-cooking fruits, delicate vegetables, and shellfish.

To ensure even cooking, avoid threading foods tightly together on the skewer. Leave about ¼ inch of breathing room between individual pieces to allow the heat to crisp all the edges.

Note: You can also place the kebabs on an aluminum foil–lined baking sheet coated with cooking spray. Preheat the broiler, place the kebabs 2 to 3 inches from the heat source, and broil until light brown, 5 to 6 minutes.

When removing hot food from the skewers, always wear oven mitts. Hold one end of the skewer with one hand and with the other hand grab the food with short-handled tongs or a pot holder. Pull the food off onto serving plates.

grilled ginseng chicken with lime-peanut sauce

I have to credit my friends in Singapore for this dish. They invited me to a gathering at which they served a memorable grilled chicken with a pungent lime-peanut sauce. In my version, I coat the chicken with cooling ginseng, which gives the chicken an exotic variety of aroma and flavors. To make a full meal, serve it with whole wheat pasta and a cooling green salad.

MAKES 4 SERVINGS

4 boneless, skinless chicken breasts

1 cup Lime-Peanut Sauce (page 35)

Olive oil, as needed for brushing the grill

Contents of 4 ginseng tea bags

1. Rinse the chicken and pat dry with paper towels. Cut a couple of inch-long slashes in the chicken to allow the marinade to penetrate. Place the chicken in a shallow baking dish. Pour ½ cup of the sauce over the chicken and toss to coat. Cover and let the chicken marinate in the refrigerator overnight or for at least 4 hours.

2. Brush the grill rack generously with oil and preheat the grill to medium-low.

3. Place the ginseng tea in a shallow bowl. Remove the chicken from the marinade and dip each piece in the tea to coat thoroughly. Discard the marinade. Place the chicken on the rack and grill until cooked through and no longer pink, 15 to 20 minutes per side, turning once halfway through.

4. In a small saucepan, bring the remaining ½ cup sauce to a boil. Drizzle over the chicken and serve hot.

spicy sesame ribs

Marinated ribs become tender and juicy, and a Spicy Sesame Sauce gives them a delightful Asian accent. When grilled, the intoxicating aroma of the sauce will arouse every diner's anticipation. This is my evolved version of traditional American barbecued ribs.

MAKES 4 SERVINGS

2 pounds baby back ribs

2 cups Spicy Sesame Sauce (page 37) or store-bought Asian sauce

Olive oil, as needed for brushing the grill

2 tablespoons white sesame seeds, toasted (see page 32)

1. Rinse the ribs, pat dry with paper towels, and slice them into individual pieces.

2. Combine the ribs and sauce in a large container. Cover and marinate in the refrigerator overnight or for at least 4 hours.

3. Brush the grill rack generously with oil and preheat the grill to medium-low. Remove the ribs from the marinade. Reserve the marinade.

4. Place the ribs on the rack and grill, basting frequently with the remaining marinade. Stop basting 5 minutes before the ribs are done. Discard any unused marinade. Grill the ribs until they are golden brown, tender, and no longer pink inside, 12 to 15 minutes per side. Sprinkle with the sesame seeds and serve hot.

grape leaf–wrapped tofu in thai sauce

Freezing and thawing changes tofu's consistency. It becomes less likely to crumble. After pressing out the excess water in the tofu, it readily absorbs other flavors. In this recipe, the scent of the ginseng and the taste of the fresh grape leaves complement the pungent peanut sauce, transforming the mild tofu into an unforgettable sensation.

MAKES 4 TO 6 SERVINGS

One 16-ounce block extra-firm tofu

1 cup Essential Thai Peanut Sauce (page 41)

6 cups water

16 fresh large grape leaves or jarred grape leaves

1 lemongrass stalk, bottom 6 inches only, minced

2 tablespoons American ginseng, minced, or the contents of 2 ginseng tea bags

Olive oil, as needed for brushing the grill

1. Place the tofu in its package in the freezer overnight. Let it thaw in the refrigerator or in a bowl of cold water. Drain the package water from the tofu. Rinse the tofu under cold running water.

2. Place the tofu on a cutting board and press out any excess water. Cut the tofu into 4-inch cubes.

3. In a medium bowl, toss the tofu with the sauce to coat. Cover and marinate in the refrigerator for 3 hours, turning once.

4. In a large pot, bring the water to a boil. Add the grape leaves and boil until the leaves soften and turn bright green, 1 to 2 minutes. Drain the leaves in a colander.

5. Lay two leaves with a 2-inch overlap on an 8-inch-square piece of aluminum foil. Place one piece of tofu in the middle and sprinkle on some lemongrass and ginseng. Tightly fold over the four corners of the leaves. Repeat with the remaining ingredients.

6. Brush the grill rack generously with oil and preheat the grill to medium. Place the grape leaf–wrapped tofu on the rack and grill until the tofu is heated through, about 8 minutes per side. Serve hot.

beef and vegetable kebabs

Like me, this dish has traveled a long way. In the '80s, when I worked as a translator for China's National Seismology Bureau, I went to Nanzhou, a northern city near the Silk Road. It was there that I first tasted beef-vegetable kebabs in a Middle Eastern restaurant. The meat was tender and burst with flavors.

In this dish, I marinate the beef with pungent spices, such as chile, garlic, and lemongrass and finish it with Western-inspired Sun-Dried Tomato–Green Tea Sauce. For a seafood or vegetarian version, replace the beef with one pound of sea scallops, shrimp, or cubed extra-firm tofu.

MAKES 8 KEBABS

1 pound beef tenderloin, cut into 1-inch cubes

1 fresh red chile pepper, minced

1 tablespoon finely minced lemongrass, white part only

3 garlic cloves, minced

Contents of 2 green tea bags

2 tablespoons low-sodium soy sauce

1 tablespoon hot-pepper sesame oil

1 tablespoon fresh lemon juice

Olive oil, as needed for brushing the grill

1 medium white onion, cut into 1-inch pieces

1 medium yellow squash, cut into 1-inch pieces

½ pound cherry tomatoes

1 cup Sun-Dried Tomato–Green Tea Sauce (page 28)

1. Place the beef cubes in a bowl with the chile, lemongrass, garlic, tea, soy sauce, sesame oil, and lemon juice. Toss to coat. Cover and refrigerate for 3 to 4 hours or overnight.

2. Soak 8 bamboo skewers in cold water for at least 30 minutes. Brush the grill rack generously with olive oil and preheat the grill to medium-low. Alternately thread the beef, onion, squash, and tomatoes onto the skewers.

3. Place the kebabs on the rack and grill on both sides until the beef is no longer pink and the vegetables are tender and lightly browned, 6 to 7 minutes per side. Serve with the Sund-Dried Tomato–Green Tea Sauce.

NOTE: To cook indoors, see "All about Kebabs," page 162.

dumpling burgers with grilled vegetables

One day, as I was preparing filling to make dumplings for guests, I realized that I didn't have enough dumpling skins. My son reached into the bowl and began fashioning the filling into patties. We grilled our "dumpling burgers" and sandwiched them between fresh vegetables. When all of the guests asked for the recipe, I knew I had to include this dish in my cookbook.

MAKES 8 SERVINGS

2 pounds lean ground beef or turkey

1 cup fresh basil leaves, finely minced

1 fresh red chile pepper, finely minced

3½ tablespoons olive oil, plus more as needed for brushing the grill

½ teaspoon salt, plus more as needed

1 large zucchini, cut into 1-inch-thick slices

2 medium tomatoes, preferably heirloom or orange, cut into 1-inch-thick slices

2 tablespoons balsamic vinegar

1 tablespoon fresh lemon juice

Toasted whole wheat bread or hamburger buns (optional)

1. In a large bowl, mix the meat with the basil, chile, and 1½ tablespoons of the oil and season with a bit of salt. Cover and refrigerate for 10 minutes.

2. In a large bowl, gently toss the zucchini and tomatoes with the remaining 2 tablespoons oil, the vinegar, lemon juice, and ½ teaspoon salt.

3. Brush the grill rack generously with oil and preheat the grill to medium. Divide the meat mixture into 8 equal portions and flatten each with your hands to make a patty. Grill the hamburgers until the meat is cooked through, turning once, about 2 minutes per side.

4. Grill the zucchini and tomatoes, turning them frequently until the zucchini softens and both the zucchini and tomatoes are browned on both sides.

5. **TO SERVE:** Place the hamburgers between the grilled vegetables and serve with or without toasted bread or buns.

lamb kebabs with curry-peanut sauce

I didn't eat lamb often until a recent visit to my Chinese doctor for my tennis elbow. After taking my pulse and inspecting my tongue, he surprised me by instructing me to eat lamb and other yang foods, to help nourish my blood and invigorate circulation. After a change in diet, rest, and a few acupuncture treatments, I'm back to the badminton court, and lamb has become one of my favorite sources of protein.

The combination of lamb and ginseng will stimulate energy levels and strengthen your *chi*. Tender lamb is ideal for these kebabs. Serve them with whole grain on cold days or a cooling green salad to balance their yang during summer.

MAKES 4 SERVINGS

1 pound lamb, cut into 1-inch cubes

1 fresh red chile pepper, minced

4 lemongrass stalks, white part only, finely chopped

3 garlic cloves, minced

Contents of 2 ginseng tea bags

1 tablespoon extra-virgin olive oil, plus more as needed for brushing the grill

Salt

1 cup Curry-Peanut Sauce (page 34)

1. Place the lamb in a medium bowl. Add the chile, lemongrass, garlic, ginseng, oil, and salt and toss well to combine. Cover and refrigerate for 3 to 4 hours or overnight.

2. Soak 8 bamboo skewers in cold water for at least 30 minutes. Brush the grill rack generously with oil and preheat the grill to medium-low. Thread the lamb cubes onto the skewers. Reserve the marinade.

3. Brush the kebabs with the reserved marinade and place on the grill rack. Grill on both sides until browned, brushing with marinade again before turning, 5 to 6 minutes per side. Stop basting 5 minutes before the kebabs are done. Discard the unused marinade. Serve with the Curry-Peanut Sauce.

NOTE: To cook the kebabs indoors see "All about Kebabs," page 162.

steak with spicy sesame sauce

One summer, when I visited friends in a small town in Colorado, I offered to cook dinner for them. In their local health food store, I found juicy steaks and the ingredients for the sauce. I then stopped at their farmers' market and bought fresh mushrooms and chile peppers. To make this dish into a complete meal, I served it with Couscous-Fennel Salad with Oranges and Almonds (page 96). The next day, I tossed the leftover sliced steak with noodles and vegetables for a quick, delicious lunch.

MAKES 4 SERVINGS

steak

Four 4-ounce boneless steaks (sirloin, flank steak, or London broil)

⅓ cup Spicy Sesame Sauce (page 37)

Olive oil, as needed for brushing the grill

topping

2 teaspoons extra-virgin olive oil, plus more as needed for brushing the grill

3 tablespoons chopped fresh ginger

4 green onions, green and white parts, chopped

½ cup fresh mushrooms, chopped

2 fresh red chile peppers, seeded and minced

Salt

Freshly ground black pepper

1. **TO PREPARE THE STEAK:** Trim any fat from the steaks and place in a shallow container.

2. Add the sauce to the steaks, cover, and marinate in the refrigerator for 30 minutes.

3. Brush the grill rack generously with oil and preheat the grill to high. Grill the steaks until they reach the desired doneness, 7 to 8 minutes per side, basting once or twice with the marinade. Stop basting about 5 minutes before the steak has finished cooking. Discard the unused marinade.

4. **TO MAKE THE TOPPING:** Combine all of the ingredients in a nonstick grill pan and grill over medium-high heat until the vegetables are soft and fragrant, about 2 minutes.

5. Garnish the steaks with the topping and serve hot.

grilled orange shrimp

This recipe is reminiscent of my sister-in-law's stir-fried orange shrimp, which I couldn't stop thinking about on the flight home from a recent visit to China. I decided to experiment with my own version. I marinated shrimp overnight with pungent orange, ginger, and chile to infuse it with flavor before grilling. The result was worth every bit of effort. To make it into a healthy meal, serve it on top of whole wheat pasta along with a simple green salad.

MAKES 6 SERVINGS

marinade

½ cup fresh orange juice

2 teaspoons grated orange zest

2 tablespoons seasoned rice vinegar

2 tablespoons soy sauce

1 tablespoon extra-virgin olive oil, plus more as needed for brushing the grill

1 tablespoon minced fresh ginger

1 green onion, minced

2 teaspoons chopped fresh cilantro leaves

1 fresh red chile pepper, minced

1 pound large shrimp, peeled and deveined

Olive oil, as needed for brushing the grill

4 large oranges, peeled and cut into chunks

1. **TO MAKE THE MARINADE:** Combine the orange juice, orange zest, rice vinegar, soy sauce, oil, ginger, green onion, cilantro, and chile in a bowl.

2. Add the shrimp to the marinade and toss to coat. Cover and refrigerate for 30 minutes or overnight.

3. Brush the grill rack generously with oil and preheat the grill to medium-low. Remove the shrimp from the marinade, and reserve the marinade.

4. Add the shrimp to a grill tray and grill, turning and basting with the reserved marinade, until the shrimp turn pink, 5 to 7 minutes per side. Stop basting 2 minutes before the shrimp are done. Discard the unused marinade. Add the oranges and toss to combine. Grill just until the oranges are warmed through.

almond trout with mango-ginger salsa

When I lived in Colorado, most of the available seafood was frozen, except fresh brook trout. This quickly became one of my family's favorite seafood dishes.

To select the best trout, look for fish with clear, bright eyes, and avoid those with eyes that appear milky or sunken. Other fatty, delicate fish, such as salmon, bluefish, steelhead trout, or arctic char, make for good substitutes.

MAKES 4 SERVINGS

2 tablespoons extra-virgin olive oil, plus more as needed for brushing the grill

4 whole (12 ounces each) trout, cleaned with tails and heads on, rinsed and dried

Salt

Freshly ground black pepper

2 green onions, white parts only, thinly shredded

1 tablespoon thinly shredded fresh ginger

1 medium red bell pepper, seeded and cut into 1 x 4-inch strips

1 medium yellow bell pepper, seeded and cut into 1 x 4-inch strips

¼ cup slivered almonds, for garnish

½ cup Mango-Ginger Salsa (page 40)

1. Brush the grill rack generously with oil and preheat the grill to medium-low. Cut three diagonal slashes on each side of the fish. Rub the fish inside and out with salt and pepper. Stuff the slashes and the body cavity with the green onions and ginger.

2. Brush the outside of the fish with the oil. Place the trout on the grill rack and cook until browned on the outside and opaque close to the bone, 5 to 8 minutes per side.

3. As the trout cooks, grill the bell peppers until tender and browned, 5 to 7 minutes.

4. Arrange the grilled bell peppers around the fish. Garnish the fish with the almonds. Serve with the Mango-Ginger Salsa.

NOTE: This recipe also works well when cooked on a stove-top grill pan.

salmon with sun-dried tomato–green tea sauce

My longtime love for salmon intensified after one of my badminton partners, a retired doctor, couldn't stop talking about its health benefits. I learned that our bodies don't produce omega-3 fatty acids, so we must get them from supplements or foods like oily fish, dark leafy vegetables, olive oil, and nuts.

Oily fish, such as salmon, are high in omega-3 fatty acids, which can protect against heart disease, help maintain vision by protecting the retina, and help brain cells transmit electrical signals. The peach and Sun-Dried Tomato–Green Tea Sauce adds a sweet, exotic touch to this simple salmon dish.

MAKES 4 SERVINGS

salmon

Four 6-ounce skinless salmon fillets

2 cups Sun-Dried Tomato–Green Tea Sauce (page 28)

1 tablespoon extra-virgin olive oil, plus more as needed for brushing the grill

garnish

¼ cup diced red onion

¼ cup peeled, pitted, and diced peach

¼ cup chopped watercress

1 tablespoon balsamic vinegar

Salt

Freshly ground black pepper

1. **TO PREPARE THE SALMON:** Place the salmon fillets in a shallow pan. Spoon the sauce over the salmon and turn to coat. Cover and refrigerate overnight or for at least 4 hours, turning twice.

2. Brush the grill rack generously with oil and preheat the grill to medium-high.

3. **TO MAKE THE GARNISH:** Place the onion, peach, and watercress in a bowl. Toss with the vinegar and oil. Cover and refrigerate while the salmon cooks.

(continued)

4. Remove the salmon from the marinade, and reserve the marinade. Season the salmon with salt and pepper on both sides.

5. Place the salmon on the grill rack and grill until opaque throughout, 4 to 6 minutes per side, basting occasionally with the reserved marinade. Stop basting about 2 minutes before the salmon has finished cooking. Discard the unused marinade.

6. Arrange the fish on four plates and garnish each with the onion, peach, and watercress just before serving.

NOTE: To cook the salmon in the oven, preheat the broiler. Line a baking sheet with a piece of aluminum foil coated with cooking spray. Broil the fish, 2 to 3 inches from the heat source, for 4 to 6 minutes per side, until the fish flakes when tested with a fork.

salmon steaks with mango-ginger salsa

At my public speaking events, a common question the audience asks is, "What are your favorite foods?" This one is among the dishes I name. It is common knowledge that salmon is high in omega-3 fatty acids, which are good for the heart. It is also one of the best dietary sources of vitamin D.

When grilled, the high heat sears the salmon, and the sesame seeds form a thin crust that seals in the flavor and adds a nutty taste and a crunchy texture. The fish can be served on top of a fresh garden salad, making for a satisfying meal.

MAKES 4 SERVINGS

2 teaspoons Savory Green Tea Oil (page 42) or extra-virgin olive oil, plus more olive oil as needed for brushing the grill

1½ teaspoons crushed red pepper flakes

2 teaspoons minced fresh ginger

2 teaspoons light brown sugar

2 teaspoons ground cumin

1 teaspoon dried thyme leaves

1 teaspoon garlic salt

1 tablespoon fresh lemon juice

Four 6-ounce skinless salmon fillets

1 cup black sesame seeds, toasted (see page 32)

½ cup Mango-Ginger Salsa (page 40)

1. Brush the grill rack generously with oil and preheat the grill to medium-high. In a small bowl, mix the red pepper flakes, ginger, sugar, cumin, thyme, garlic salt, oil, and lemon juice.

2. Using your hands, rub both sides of the fillets with the spice mixture and then coat them with ½ cup of the sesame seeds.

3. Place the fillets on the grill rack and grill, turning once, 5 to 8 minutes per side. Divide the salmon equally among four plates. Top with the remaining sesame seeds and serve hot, accompanied by the Mango-Ginger Salsa.

scallop, onion, and colorful pepper kebabs

Growing up, I only had dried scallops, and they were considered a rare delicacy. When I saw giant, fresh, shiny scallops in stores, I was overjoyed. Grilling is my favorite method of cooking scallops because it brings out their sweetness. In this dish, the sour, salty, and pungent Lime-Soy-Ginger Sauce enhances the flavor of the scallops beautifully.

These kebabs cook quickly and are best served hot, so place them all on the grill at the same time. The cooling watercress balances the yang in this dish.

MAKES 4 SERVINGS

1 cup Lime-Soy-Ginger Sauce (page 32)

1 pound sea scallops

Olive oil, as needed for brushing the grill

1 large red onion, cut into chunks

1 medium yellow bell pepper, seeded and cut into large pieces

1 medium red bell pepper, seeded and cut into large pieces

½ cup minced watercress

Rice, noodles, or grilled tortillas, for serving

1. Place ½ cup of the sauce and the scallops in a bowl and toss to coat. Cover and marinate in the refrigerator for 1 to 2 hours.

2. Soak four 12-inch bamboo skewers in cold water for at least 30 minutes. Brush the grill rack generously with oil and preheat the grill to medium.

3. Drain the scallops, and reserve the marinade. Alternately thread the scallops, onion, and bell peppers onto the skewers; brush with the reserved marinade.

4. Place the kebabs on the grill rack and cook, turning and basting with the remaining reserved marinade, until the scallops turn opaque, 3 to 4 minutes per side. Stop basting 2 minutes before the kebabs are done. Discard the unused marinade

5. Divide the skewers equally among four plates and garnish with the watercress. Bring the remaining ½ cup sauce to a boil and serve as a dipping sauce. Serve with rice, noodles, or grilled tortillas.

NOTE: To cook the kebabs indoors see "All about Kebabs," page 162.

sea bass with grilled bananas

The first time I tasted grilled bananas and fish was in Vietnam. I couldn't get a translation for the name of the white fish I was served, but after much experimentation, I found that sea bass has a similar flavor. Grilled bananas offer a warm, sweet, and rich counterpart to the tender fish. Peel the bananas just before serving. This dish makes for a perfect hot summer night's meal.

MAKES 4 SERVINGS

Four 6-ounce sea bass fillets
1 cup Chile-Garlic Sauce (page 27)
Olive oil, as needed for brushing the grill
2 large bananas

4½ teaspoons unsalted butter, melted
1 cup Papaya-Mango Salsa (page 39), for garnish

1. Place the fish in a shallow dish, cover with the sauce, and marinate for 1 hour in the refrigerator.

2. Brush the grill rack generously with oil and preheat the grill to medium-low. Remove the fish from the marinade and discard the marinade. Grill the fish until it flakes when tested with a fork, 4 to 6 minutes per side.

3. Grill the bananas in the peels alongside the fish until soft, about 4 minutes. Using a heatproof spatula, transfer the fish and bananas to a serving plate. Peel the bananas and cut into big pieces.

4. Drizzle the melted butter over the bananas, and garnish the fish with the Papaya-Mango Salsa. Serve hot.

the
art of
steaming

Even after all these years, I still frequently dream about how the delicious aroma of steaming food enveloped our small family apartment in Wuhan.

Steaming is one of the most popular cooking techniques in Asia, as the average kitchen is not equipped with an oven. While stir-frying is considered a yang cooking method, steaming is yin. A surprising variety of foods, such as seafood, meat, vegetables, custards, dumplings, and even desserts, can be steamed. It is the ideal technique for those who want to cook and enjoy a quick and healthful meal. The key is to use only the freshest ingredients.

My fondness for steamed food lies in its clean, delicate tastes. Steaming works by suspending food over boiling water. The hot moisture evaporating from the boiling water surrounds and cooks the food, allowing the ingredients to retain all their vitamins, minerals, moisture, and flavors.

The traditional approach to steaming is to set a bamboo basket steamer inside a wok. However, you can also use a Pyrex pie plate or other heatproof dish that fits into a metal vegetable steamer. Another method is to bring water to a boil in a large pot, then place the dish of food in a metal steamer basket or on a round cake rack. Be sure to use a dish with deep sloping sides to prevent the sauce from spilling, and to make it easier to remove after cooking. The general guides on the next page will ensure your successful steaming.

general guides to steaming

- Always place the food on a heat-resistant dish that is slightly smaller than the steamer.

- Bring the water to a boil before placing the plate of food to be steamed.

- Once the plate is in the steamer, cover the steamer, so the food heats evenly and efficiently.

- Dumplings can go directly on a rack or in a steamer basket lined with thinly sliced carrots or with cabbage leaves to prevent sticking.

- Steaming requires lots of water. Check the water level as the food cooks, and replenish water as necessary. Keep a teakettle full of hot water next to the steamer.

- Don't submerge the food. Keep it above the water level at all times.

- Don't crowd the food. Make sure there is enough space between items so that the steam can circulate evenly.

- Wear oven mitts when adding food to and removing food from a steamer. Waterproof silicone mitts work the best.

- Always carefully lift the lid away from you so that your hands and face are not exposed to scalding steam.

green beans with golden raisins

This recipe exemplifies how Western ingredients—raisins and Parmesan cheese—can be combined with Eastern flavors such as sesame seeds and fragrant tea. Chinese doctors believe green beans tone the kidneys and strengthen the spleen. Raisins are a good source of potassium, a mineral shown to lower high blood pressure. Golden raisins are a vibrant complement to the green beans and black sesame seeds, but other varieties can be substituted.

MAKES 6 SERVINGS

2 green or white tea bags

2 pounds green beans, trimmed

¼ cup golden raisins

3 tablespoons rice vinegar

1 tablespoon sesame oil

2 tablespoons black sesame seeds, toasted (see page 32)

¼ cup shaved Parmigiano-Reggiano cheese, for garnish

1. Bring water to a boil over high heat in a covered steamer or pot large enough to hold a 10-inch glass pie plate. Add the tea bags to the water. Arrange the green beans on the pie plate.

2. Wearing oven mitts, carefully place the pie plate into the steamer. Cover, lower the heat to medium-high, and steam until the beans are bright green, about 4 minutes.

3. Using oven mitts, carefully lift the lid of the steamer away from you and sprinkle the raisins onto the green beans. Re-cover and steam for 1 minute more. Using oven mitts, carefully lift the lid of the steamer away from you, and remove the pie plate from the steamer.

3. In a large salad bowl, toss the green beans and raisins with the rice vinegar, sesame oil, and sesame seeds.

4. Garnish with the shaved cheese and serve immediately.

steamed eggplant with garlic and chopped olives

During the Cultural Revolution when we were low on rationed oil, my grand-mother would steam eggplant. Once steamed, she flavored it with fresh garlic, chile pepper, pickled vegetables, and a few drops of oil. To make it even healthier, I use olive oil instead of cottonseed oil, the only oil available to us at the time. Chopped olives make a nice substitute for the pickled vegetables. The result is a flavorful, delicious dish that won't make you feel a bit deprived.

The best Asian eggplants are firm and lavender in color. They are more tender and less bitter and seedy than their Mediterranean cousins. Do not oversteam eggplant or it will lose its texture.

MAKES 6 SERVINGS

3 medium Asian eggplants, halved

½ cup pitted green olives, roughly chopped

4 garlic cloves, minced

1 small fresh red chile pepper, minced

2 green onions, chopped

2 tablespoons olive oil

2 tablespoons balsamic vinegar

1½ teaspoons fresh lemon juice

1. Bring water to a boil over high heat in a covered steamer or pot large enough to hold a 10-inch glass pie plate. Arrange the eggplant halves on the pie plate.

2. Wearing oven mitts, carefully place the pie plate into the steamer. Cover, lower the heat to medium-high, and steam until the eggplant is tender when tested with a fork, about 5 minutes. Using oven mitts, carefully lift the lid of the steamer away from you. Using tongs, transfer the eggplant to a bowl.

3. Whisk together the olives, garlic, chile, green onions, oil, vinegar, and lemon juice in a small bowl.

4. Toss the eggplant with the olive sauce and serve.

steamed asparagus with miso-sesame sauce

Steaming is the best cooking method to preserve the nutrients in food. TCM views asparagus as a cooling vegetable with detoxifying and diuretic effects. In China, white asparagus is considered a delicacy and is reserved for important guests, yet its green counterpart works just as well.

MAKES 4 SERVINGS

1 pound white or green asparagus spears, woody lower portion of stems removed

½ cup Miso-Sesame Sauce (page 33)

2 tablespoons minced fresh flat-leaf parsley, for garnish

2 tablespoons seeded and minced red bell pepper, for garnish

1. Bring water to a boil over high heat in a covered steamer or pot large enough to hold a 10-inch glass pie plate. Arrange the asparagus spears on the pie plate.

2. Wearing oven mitts, carefully place the pie plate into the steamer. Cover, lower the heat to medium, and steam the asparagus until bright green and just tender when pierced with the point of a knife, 4 to 5 minutes.

3. Using oven mitts, carefully lift the lid of the steamer away from you, and remove the pie plate from the steamer. Drizzle the asparagus with the sauce and garnish with the parsley and bell pepper just before serving.

Tofu Stuffed with Ginger Crabmeat (left)
and Pearl Meatballs (right; page 208)

tofu stuffed with ginger crabmeat

There are a multitude of methods for preparing tofu, as it has long been the main protein source in many Asian countries. In this recipe, blocks of tofu become small containers for the crabmeat filling.

The original version, which I ate at a famous Buddhist temple next to the Yangtze River, uses minced wild mushrooms and onions for the filling. I altered it to satisfy my craving for fresh seafood and meat.

MAKES 4 SERVINGS

Two 16-ounce blocks extra-firm tofu

filling

¼ cup fresh lump crabmeat, minced

4 ounces ground pork

1 tablespoon cornstarch

1½ teaspoons minced fresh ginger

½ cup Chile-Garlic Sauce (page 27)

2 tablespoons fish sauce

1 tablespoon rice wine

1½ teaspoons sesame oil

¼ teaspoon ground white pepper

vegetable garnish

2 teaspoons olive oil

½ cup shredded leek

½ cup shredded carrots

1 tablespoon fresh lemon juice

1 tablespoon soy sauce

1. Lay the tofu on a cutting board. Cut the tofu horizontally and then lengthwise vertically to make 4 blocks. Carve a round out of the top of each block, to about half the depth of the block. Using a small spoon, scoop out more tofu from each round to deepen the hollow. Reserve the scooped-out tofu.

2. **TO MAKE THE FILLING:** In a bowl, mix together the scooped-out tofu with the crabmeat, pork, cornstarch, ginger, Chile-Garlic Sauce, fish sauce, rice wine, sesame oil, and white pepper.

(continued)

3. Bring water to a boil over high heat in a covered steamer or pot large enough to hold a 10-inch glass pie plate. Fill each piece of tofu with about 1 tablespoon of the filling. (You will not use all the filling.) Arrange the stuffed tofu on the pie plate.

4. Wearing oven mitts, carefully place the pie plate into the steamer. Cover, lower the heat to medium, and steam for 20 minutes.

5. **MEANWHILE, PREPARE THE VEGETABLE GARNISH:** Heat the olive oil in a wok or nonstick skillet and sauté the remaining filling for 2 minutes. Add the leek and carrots and cook, stirring, until the vegetables are tender, about 2 minutes. Add the lemon juice and soy sauce.

6. Using oven mitts, carefully lift the lid of the steamer away from you and remove the pie plate from the steamer. Arrange the tofu on a serving plate and garnish with the vegetable mixture on top. Serve hot.

COOKING WITH AN ASIAN ACCENT

green tea–steamed shrimp dumplings

Every region in China has its own local specialties, yet no matter where you go, you can always find delicious dumplings like these. Traditionally, the steamer is greased with oil to prevent the food from sticking. I've come up with a simple, healthy method that achieves the same result, placing each dumpling on a disk of thinly sliced carrot. Once cooked, the carrots make a sweet, tender accompaniment to the green tea–infused dumplings.

If your steamer is not large enough to steam all the dumplings at one time, you can either use stackable steamer baskets or steam the dumplings in batches.

MAKES 40 DUMPLINGS

filling

2 teaspoons extra-virgin olive oil

1 tablespoon minced fresh ginger

1 small leek, minced (about 1 cup)

¾ pound large shrimp, peeled, deveined, and cut into ¼-inch pieces

1 tablespoon rice wine

¼ teaspoon freshly ground black pepper

Dash of salt

dumplings

40 wonton wrappers

2 large, thick carrots, sliced into ¼-inch-thick rounds

4 green tea bags

Chile-Garlic Sauce (page 27), for dipping

1. **TO MAKE THE FILLING:** Heat the oil in a wok or nonstick skillet over medium-high heat. Add the ginger and leek and sauté for about 2 minutes, or until soft.

2. Combine the leek mixture with the shrimp, rice wine, pepper, and salt in a large bowl and mix well.

(continued)

3. **PREPARE A SPACE FOR ASSEMBLING:** Arrange a bowl of cold water, the won-
    ton wrappers, and the bowl with the filling near a steamer basket. Cover the
    wrappers with a moist paper towel to prevent them from drying out as you
    work.

4. Arrange the carrot slices in a single layer in the steamer.

5. **TO ASSEMBLE THE DUMPLINGS:** Working with one wrapper at a time, dip all
    four edges into the cold water. Holding the wrapper flat on your palm, place
    about 1 teaspoon of filling in the center of the wrapper. Bring the four cor-
    ners of the wrapper up over the filling. Pinch the edges together tightly. Set
    each dumpling on a carrot slice, leaving a little space between each dumpling.
    Repeat with the remaining wrappers and filling.

6. Fill a large pot or wok with water for steaming. Bring the water to a boil. Add
    the tea bags to the water. Set the steamer in the pot. The water should not
    touch the steamer. Cover and steam until the dumpling skins are translucent,
    10 to 12 minutes. Serve warm with the Chile-Garlic Sauce.

green tea and orange chicken

I learned this dry steam-cooking method from my sister-in-law in Wuhan. The steam comes from the leafy vegetables, while the tea, rice, and orange peel produce an intoxicating smoke, making this dish a cross between steaming and smoking. I have used the same method to cook fish and tofu, accompanied by various sauces. The results are always satisfying.

Be sure to line your pan with aluminum foil. It will make cleanup a snap. I've found that an old cast-iron pan or skillet works best. Do not use a non-stick pan for this recipe.

MAKES 4 SERVINGS

4 medium boneless, skinless chicken breasts

1 cup Lime-Soy-Ginger Sauce (page 32)

3 large lettuce leaves

⅓ cup loose green tea or the contents of 6 tea bags

½ cup white rice

½ cup fresh orange or lemon peel, chopped

2 tablespoons sugar

2 cups of mixed, colorful, leafy salad greens such as spinach, mustard greens, or romaine lettuce, for serving

1. Cut 1-inch-deep diagonal slashes on one side of the chicken breasts, spacing them about 2 inches apart. Place the breasts slashed side down into a large bowl with half of the sauce. Cover and refrigerate for at least 30 minutes, or overnight for best flavor.

2. Line the bottom of an old large cast-iron pan with aluminum foil and then line it with the lettuce leaves. Mix together the green tea, rice, orange peel, and sugar on top of the lettuce leaves.

3. Place a steamer basket into the pan and place the chicken breasts on it. Tightly cover the pan with foil and a lid. Cook over medium heat for 25 to 30 minutes, or until the chicken is opaque and cooked through. Arrange the chicken atop a bed of the greens. Drizzle with the remaining sauce and serve hot.

tea-steamed broccoli

I always feel sorry when I see children being encouraged to eat broccoli that has been steamed into a bland mush. I've found that when the broccoli is deliciously flavored and well presented, children eat their vegetables voluntarily. In this dish, the tea, miso, and sesame give the broccoli an exotic flavor, and the minced red bell peppers brighten the presentation.

The stronger black tea adds warm overtones to the broccoli's essence. For a milder flavor, try green or white tea.

MAKES 4 SERVINGS

2 tablespoons white miso

4½ teaspoons black sesame seeds, toasted (see page 32)

2 tablespoons fresh lemon juice

½ cup soy milk or rice milk

4 black tea bags

1 pound broccoli, cut into florets

2 tablespoons seeded and minced red bell pepper, for garnish

1. In a small bowl, whisk together the miso, sesame seeds, and lemon juice. Slowly whisk in the soy milk until smooth. Add more liquid if you prefer a thinner sauce. Set aside.

2. Bring water to a boil over high heat in a covered steamer or pot large enough to hold a 10-inch glass pie plate. Add the tea bags to the water. Arrange the broccoli florets on the pie plate.

3. Wearing oven mitts, carefully place the pie plate into the steamer. Cover and steam until the broccoli is bright green and just tender, about 5 minutes.

4. Using oven mitts, carefully lift the lid of the steamer away from you. Using tongs, transfer the broccoli to a serving dish. Drizzle with the sauce and garnish with the red bell pepper.

steamed egg custard with prosciutto and green onions

In both Japan and China, there are many variations of egg custards. The traditional version is often flavored with dry, salty seafood and pickled vegetables. In my East-Meets-West variation, I use prosciutto to give the dish a savory Western flair. The two most famous types of Italian prosciutto are prosciutto di Parma, which has a slightly nutty flavor, and prosciutto di San Daniele, which is darker in color and has a mild, sweeter flavor. I prefer prosciutto di San Daniele for this dish.

The egg mixture cooks slowly over simmering water, yielding a moist custard perfect for a light dinner or lunch.

MAKES 4 SERVINGS

1 large, fresh shiitake mushroom cap, minced

1 tablespoon chopped fresh cilantro leaves

1 tablespoon low-sodium soy sauce

1 teaspoon minced fresh ginger

1 tablespoon rice vinegar

4 large organic eggs, lightly beaten

¼ cup finely chopped prosciutto (about ½ ounce)

¼ cup minced green onions

1 teaspoon toasted sesame oil

3 cups hot cooked basmati rice

1. Bring water to a boil over high heat in a covered steamer or pot large enough to hold a 10-inch glass pie plate.

2. Spray the pie plate with olive oil cooking spray.

3. Whisk together the mushroom, cilantro, soy sauce, ginger, rice vinegar, and eggs in a bowl and pour the mixture into the pie plate.

4. Wearing oven mitts, carefully place the pie plate into the steamer. Cover and steam for 3 minutes.

5. Using oven mitts, carefully lift the lid of the steamer away from you and sprinkle the custard with the prosciutto and green onions. Re-cover and steam for 3 minutes more, or until a knife inserted in the center comes out clean.

6. Using oven mitts, carefully lift the lid of the steamer away from you, and remove the plate from the steamer. Drizzle the custard with the sesame oil and cut into 4 wedges. Serve over the rice.

shrimp custard with ginger and shiitake mushrooms

During a trip to Japan, my host took me to a restaurant known for its tea and its twenty-course meals. Most courses were just two-bite morsels, but they were beautifully presented. Egg custard was the first dish served and remained my favorite of the evening.

The key to making perfect egg custard is to avoid oversteaming. Remove it from the heat as soon as the egg mixture sets, and barely trembles when the dish is touched, so it won't be spongy. You can find dashi—fish stock with seaweed—at Asian grocery stores. Steam the egg custard in a 3-or 4-cup heatproof bowl or in ramekins for single servings. This dish makes for a memorable opener for a dinner gathering.

MAKES 4 SERVINGS

¼ pound small shrimp, peeled, deveined, and chopped

¼ cup minced fresh shiitake mushroom caps

2 tablespoons minced fresh ginger

4½ teaspoons soy sauce

1 tablespoon rice wine or dry sherry

4 large organic eggs, lightly beaten

1¼ cups warm dashi or chicken stock

1 tablespoon soy sauce

2 teaspoons sesame oil

Small, edible, organic, pesticide-free flower petals, such as violets, for garnish (optional)

1. Mix the shrimp, mushrooms, ginger, soy sauce, and rice wine in a bowl. Cover and let marinate for 5 minutes.

2. Bring water to a boil over high heat in a covered steamer or pot large enough to hold a 9-inch shallow heatproof bowl, or four 6-ounce ramekins to make individual servings.

3. Whisk together the eggs and dashi in a large bowl. Add the shrimp mixture. Pour into the shallow heatproof bowl or divide evenly among the ramekins.

4. Wearing oven mitts, carefully place the bowl or ramekins in the steamer. Cover, lower the heat to medium, and steam until the egg mixture sets, about 12 minutes.

5. Using oven mitts, carefully lift the lid of the steamer away from you, and remove the bowl or ramekins from the steamer. Drizzle with the soy sauce and sesame oil. Garnish with the flower petals, if using. Serve hot.

curry-coconut shrimp

Shrimp absorbs the flavors of a marinade rapidly, making this quick entrée ideal for a busy weeknight. Steaming gently cooks the shrimp and reduces the likelihood of overcooking. Regular coconut milk offers the best flavor for this dish, as the taste of light coconut milk is too subtle. I often serve it over brown rice or whole wheat noodles.

MAKES 4 SERVINGS

¼ cup unsweetened coconut milk

1½ tablespoons fish sauce

1 tablespoon fresh lemon juice

3 tablespoons seeded and finely chopped red bell pepper

1 tablespoon minced fresh cilantro leaves

1 teaspoon sugar

1 teaspoon curry powder

1½ pounds large shrimp, peeled and deveined

2 cups cooked brown rice

4 lemon wedges, for serving

Fresh cilantro sprigs, for garnish (optional)

1. Combine the coconut milk, fish sauce, lemon juice, bell pepper, minced cilantro, sugar, and curry powder in a 10-inch glass pie plate. Add the shrimp, cover, and marinate in the refrigerator for 30 minutes.

2. Bring water to a boil over high heat in a covered steamer or pot large enough to hold the pie plate. Wearing oven mitts, carefully place the pie plate into the steamer. Cover, lower the heat to medium, and steam for 4 to 6 minutes, or until the shrimp are just cooked through.

3. Using oven mitts, carefully lift the lid of the steamer away from you, and remove the pie plate from the steamer. Serve the shrimp over the brown rice. Garnish with the lemon wedges and cilantro sprigs, if using.

steamed fish with spicy ginger sauce

This delicately flavored fish dish is often served at Chinese banquets. Mild-flavored fish, such as halibut or trout fillets, works best in this recipe. As always, look for wild fish or fish from a clean water source free of hormones and antibiotics. Avoid oversteaming the fish and remove it from the heat as soon as the fish flakes when tested with a fork.

MAKES 4 SERVINGS

sauce

¼ cup fresh orange juice

2 tablespoons rice wine or dry sherry

2 tablespoons low-sodium soy sauce

1 tablespoon toasted sesame oil

1 tablespoon grated fresh ginger

½ to 1 teaspoon crushed red pepper flakes

fish

Four 6-ounce halibut or trout fillets

½ cup chopped green onions

1 tablespoon grated fresh ginger

¼ teaspoon salt

¼ teaspoon freshly ground black pepper

1 cup thinly sliced leek (about 1 large leek)

½ cup julienned carrot

½ cup seeded and julienned red bell pepper

4 sprigs fresh cilantro, chopped, for garnish

1. **TO PREPARE THE SAUCE:** Whisk together the orange juice, rice wine, soy sauce, sesame oil, ginger, and red pepper flakes in a small bowl. Set aside.

2. **TO STEAM THE FISH:** Bring water to a boil over high heat in a covered steamer or pot large enough to hold a 10-inch glass pie plate.

3. Lightly score each fish fillet by making three ¼-inch-deep crosswise slits with a knife.

4. Combine the green onions and ginger in a small bowl. Rub about 2 table-spoons of the onion-ginger mixture evenly into the slits of each fillet. Season the fillets with salt and black pepper. Set the fillets aside.

5. Mix the leek, carrot, and bell pepper in a large bowl. Arrange half of this mixture on the 10-inch glass pie plate. Pour half of the sauce over the leek mixture. Arrange the fish in a single layer over the leek mixture. Top the fish with the remaining leek mixture, and drizzle with the remaining sauce.

6. Wearing oven mitts, carefully place the pie plate into the steamer. Cover, lower the heat to medium, and steam for 10 to 12 minutes, or until the fish flakes easily when tested with a fork. Check the water level occasionally and replenish, if necessary, with boiling water.

7. Using oven mitts, carefully lift the lid of the steamer away from you, and remove the pie plate from the steamer. Garnish the fish with the cilantro and serve hot.

pearl meatballs

This is a dish from my hometown, Wuhan. It is served at all the major holidays and gatherings, as the shape of the rice balls symbolize togetherness. TCM doctors believe that both glutinous rice and pork work to tone the body's *chi*, nourish the kidneys, and restore energy.

Glutinous rice is sticky because of its high starch content, and the rice clings to the outside of the meatball like tiny, translucent "pearls." The filling can be prepared in advance and stored in a refrigerator for up to two days.

MAKES 8 SERVINGS OR 32 RICE BALLS

1½ cups uncooked white glutinous rice

1 cup Chile-Garlic Sauce (page 27), for serving

filling

2 fresh shiitake or oyster mushrooms

1 pound extra-lean ground pork

4 green onions, chopped

1 tablespoon minced fresh ginger

2 teaspoons chopped fresh cilantro leaves

3 tablespoons soy sauce

1 tablespoon sesame oil

1 teaspoon ground white pepper

1. Place the rice in a large bowl and cover with warm water. Let stand for 2 hours. Meanwhile, prepare the Chili-Garlic Sauce.

2. **TO MAKE THE PORK FILLING:** If using shiitakes, discard the stems and mince the caps. If using oyster mushrooms, mince the stems and caps.

3. Place the mushrooms, pork, green onions, ginger, cilantro, soy sauce, sesame oil, and pepper in a big bowl and mix well.

4. Drain the rice through a sieve and place it in a separate bowl.

5. Line a steamer basket with wet cheesecloth. With wet hands, roll about 1 tablespoon of the filling mixture into a small ball, then roll the ball in the rice to coat. Repeat with the remaining filling and rice. Arrange the rice balls, without crowding, on the cheesecloth.

6. Bring water to a boil over high heat in a covered steamer or pot large enough to hold the steamer basket. Wearing oven mitts, carefully place the steamer basket with the meatballs into the steamer. Cover and steam until the pork is no longer pink and the rice is tender, about 20 minutes. Check the water level occasionally and replenish, if necessary, with boiling water.

7. Using oven mitts, carefully lift the lid of the steamer away from you, and remove the steamer basket from the steamer. Arrange the rice balls on a serving plate. Serve hot with the Chili-Garlic Sauce.

shiitake mushrooms stuffed with shrimp and onions

One of the dishes my grandmother used to cook in the summer was stuffed cucumbers. In the wintertime, when cucumbers weren't available, she would use fresh mushrooms. The filling varies depending on occasion. This one contains chicken and shrimp, which are often served at Chinese New Year because they symbolize wealth and prosperity.

To save time, use ground chicken. I like to buy boneless, skinless chicken breasts at my local health-food store and ask the butcher to grind it for me. For a vegetarian version, substitute the shrimp and chicken with firm tofu. Look for shiitakes with big caps that are similar in size and save the stems for making stock.

MAKES 4 SERVINGS

6 ounces large shrimp, peeled, deveined, and chopped

4 ounces ground chicken

2 garlic cloves, minced

¼ cup chopped green onions

3 tablespoons dry-roasted peanuts

1 tablespoon grated fresh ginger

2 teaspoons cornstarch

½ teaspoon curry powder

4½ teaspoons low-sodium soy sauce

1 tablespoon rice wine

1 teaspoon toasted sesame oil

16 large, fresh shiitake mushroom caps, stemmed

1⅓ cups thinly sliced English cucumber

1⅓ cups thinly sliced carrot

1. Bring water to a boil over high heat in a covered steamer or pot large enough to hold a 10-inch glass pie plate. Combine the shrimp, chicken, garlic, green onions, peanuts, ginger, cornstarch, curry powder, soy sauce, rice wine, and

sesame oil in a food processor. Process until the mixture forms a paste. Spoon about 4½ teaspoons of the mixture evenly into each mushroom cap. Arrange the mushrooms on the pie plate.

2. Wearing oven mitts, carefully place the pie plate in the steamer. Cover and steam for 8 minutes.

3. Using oven mitts, carefully lift the lid of the steamer away from you and remove the pie plate from the steamer.

4. Arrange ⅓ cup cucumber and ⅓ cup carrot around the edge of each of four plates. Arrange 4 stuffed mushrooms in the center of each plate and serve hot.

sweet rice wrapped in lotus leaves

When I visited Xi Shuang Ban Na, a town in southeast China, I ate a dish in which uncooked rice and spices were stir-fried, then stuffed into a bamboo stalk and steamed. The combination of stir-frying and steaming gave the rice an intense flavor while retaining its moisture inside the bamboo. I wanted to re-create this dish at home, but couldn't find the stalks, so I decided to wrap the rice in lotus leaves.

When steamed, the leaves release an exotic perfume and impart a mild, sweet flavor to the rice. You can find dry lotus leaves in Asian markets, or substitute it with banana or grape leaves. Adjust the amount of filling according to the size of the leaves and don't overstuff.

MAKES 4 SERVINGS

rice

3 tablespoons extra-virgin olive oil

¼ cup minced onion

2 cups uncooked sweet brown or white rice

¼ cup bottled spicy artichoke hearts, drained and minced (juice reserved for the basil paste)

2 cups vegetable broth or rice milk

basil paste

1 cup fresh basil leaves

1 small fresh red chile pepper

¼ cup salted almonds

2 tablespoons juice from bottled spicy artichoke hearts (reserved from rice ingredients)

1 tablespoon olive oil

1½ teaspoons fresh lemon juice

Salt

Freshly ground black pepper

4 dry lotus leaves

One 12-ounce package meatless meatballs or regular meatballs

1. **TO PREPARE THE RICE:** Coat a wok or nonstick skillet with oil and place over medium-high heat. Add the onion and sauté until fragrant.

2. Add the rice and artichoke hearts and stir-fry until the rice heats through, about 3 minutes. Add the broth, reduce the heat to low, cover, and cook, removing the lid to stir occasionally, until the rice is almost soft and the broth has been absorbed, about 20 minutes. Add an additional ¼ cup water if the rice is too dry and has not softened. Remove the rice from the heat and set aside to cool slightly.

3. **TO MAKE THE BASIL PASTE:** Combine the basil, chile, almonds, artichoke juice, oil, and lemon juice in a blender and purée. Pour the purée into a small bowl and season with salt and pepper to taste.

4. Bring water to a boil over high heat in a covered steamer or pot large enough to hold a steamer basket. Dip the lotus leaves one at a time in the water until they are soft and pliable, about 30 seconds.

5. Lay a lotus leaf out on a work surface. Spread ½ cup of the rice mixture in the center of the leaf. Spread the basil paste in the middle of the rice and top with 3 meatballs. Cover with another ½ cup of rice and pack it firmly.

6. Fold the lotus leaf over to enclose the rice tightly. Turn over the bundle, so the folded side is held in place by the weight of the rice, and place it in a steamer basket. Repeat with the remaining leaves, paste, and filling.

7. Bring the water in the steamer back to a boil. Wearing oven mitts, carefully place the steamer basket with the lotus leaf bundles into the steamer. Cover and steam the bundles for 25 minutes, or until the rice has softened and heated through. Check the water level occasionally and replenish, if necessary, with boiling water.

8. Using oven mitts, carefully lift the lid of the steamer away from you and remove the steamer basket from the steamer. Serve warm.

sweet tempta-tions

Growing up during the Chinese Cultural Revolution, sugar, along with meat, toothpaste, shampoo, and many other items, was tightly rationed.

On the first day of every third month, my mother brought home variously colored tickets. I could always spot the purple one for the pound of sugar. This sugar had to last our family of five for the next three months. My mother stored the sugar in a ceramic jar inside a locked cabinet with a glass door. I spent many hours staring at the jar, daydreaming about what it would be like to have a big spoonful of sugar slowly melting on my tongue.

One day my father, a surgeon, opened the cabinet to get something, but was called away for an emergency operation. I grabbed my chance! My hands were shaking with excitement as I held the jar. When I stuffed the first spoonful in my mouth, I thought I was in heaven. After a few tablespoons, the sugar no longer tasted as sweet as I had imagined, though I still finished the whole jar. Then my tummy started to hurt, and I was disappointed. Naturally, my mother was unhappy with me when she found the empty jar. It's not a surprise that even today, I favor desserts that aren't too sweet.

TCM believes that refined sugar has a yang effect. In excess, it fuels the yang *chi*, which aggravates and harms the liver. Asian desserts tend to be lighter in texture and contain less refined sugar than their Western counterparts, as the primary ingredients in desserts are fresh fruits and sweet rice. In this chapter, I have had great fun giving popular Western desserts an Asian twist, such as Citrus Fruit Cheesecake (page 234) and Banana Bread Pudding with Vanilla-Rum-Chocolate Sauce (page 237). You will also find traditional Asian desserts like Sweet Eight-Treasure Rice Pudding (page 240), New Year's Rice Cake (page 242), and Jasmine Tea Almond Cookies (page 243).

I also take great pleasure in incorporating fresh fruit and Asian ingredients such as soy milk, green tea, and black sesame seeds into homemade smoothies and ice creams. The luscious smoothies make an excellent addition to breakfast, or a reward after a workout. The soothing ice creams make for a refreshing treat on a hot summer day and will satisfy any sweet craving. Many of them are dairy-free; if desired, you can always use dairy substitutes for the soy ingredients.

In China, the concept of food as medicine extends to desserts. Parents often encourage their children to consume sweet herbal tonics to preserve their health. Examples include Asian Beauty Tonic (page 228), Ginger–Dong Quai Chai (page 229), Hot Pomegranate Cider (page 230), and Steamed Asian Pears with Rock Sugar (page 232). In these recipes, I used easy-to-find herbs and simplified the steps to accomodate a busy Western lifestyle. With the growing interest in Eastern medicine, you can now find many Asian herbs in health food stores, Asian markets, and online.

I hope you will enjoy the sweets in this chapter after a meal, to calm the digestive system and refresh the palate. Or enjoy them as a treat during the day, as they are as satisfying as they are good for you.

ginger, mango, and yogurt smoothie

Ginger is a popular ingredient in Asian desserts. As a child, I ate many treats made with ginger—ginger candies, ginger cookies, and a sweet ginger soup. In this dish, ginger complements the sweet mango and cooling yogurt. If mango isn't available, berries, papaya, or apricot are delicious substitutes.

MAKES 4 SERVINGS

½ cup soy milk

4 quarter-size slices young fresh ginger (or 3 quarter-size slices mature fresh ginger)

2 tablespoons honey

2 medium mangoes, pitted, peeled, and cubed, and partially frozen for 15 minutes

1 cup pineapple-coconut juice

Two 6-ounce containers mango or apricot soy yogurt, or other fruit yogurt

¼ cup coconut shavings, for garnish

1. Place the soy milk, ginger, and honey in a blender and blend on medium speed for 10 seconds. Add the frozen mango cubes, pineapple-coconut juice, and yogurt.

2. Blend on medium speed until smooth and frosty, about 30 seconds. Garnish with the coconut and serve immediately or store in a tightly sealed container in the refrigerator for up to 6 hours.

coconut–soy shake

I am amused to see the recent proliferation of coconut drinks on super-market shelves, many with a high sugar content. Once you taste this simple homemade coconut soy shake, you may think twice before reaching for those canned or boxed drinks again.

Coconut, like soy, has long been praised in Asia for its medicinal uses. It is believed to strengthen the spleen and nourish the blood. Here, I pair it with soy and honey, which both sooth the lungs. You can serve this shake year-round. Add ice cubes and serve chilled on hot days and omit the ice and serve at room temperature for cold days.

MAKES 4 SERVINGS

Half a 6-ounce package silken tofu

2 cups unsweetened soy milk

½ cup unsweetened coconut milk

3 tablespoons honey

1 cup ice cubes (optional)

2 tablespoons finely chopped pistachios, for garnish

1. Combine the tofu, soy milk, coconut milk, and honey in a blender. Blend on high speed until frothy, about 2 minutes.

2. Pour into tall glasses over the ice cubes, if using. Garnish each with the pistachio. Serve immediately or store in a tightly sealed container in the refrigerator for up to 6 hours.

summer fruit refresher

I am so thrilled to see the rising popularity of farmers' markets across the country, offering fresh, locally grown fruits and vegetables. Nothing pleases me more than bringing home succulent melons from the market on a summer morning.

The cooling yin effect of American ginseng and melons is a welcome refresher on hot days. This smoothie will cleanse, rejuvenate, and energize. Drink it in the morning with breakfast, or as an afternoon pick-me-up. It also makes an ideal drink to accompany warming grilled foods.

MAKES 4 TO 6 SERVINGS

2½ cups water

2 pieces fresh or dry American ginseng, sliced

2 cups cubed seedless watermelon

2 cups cubed cantaloupe

1 cup cubed honeydew

6 ice cubes

Fresh mint leaves, for garnish

1. In a saucepan, bring the water to a boil. Add the ginseng slices, reduce the heat to low, and simmer until reduced to 2 cups, about 20 minutes. Set aside to cool.

2. Place the ginseng tea, including the ginseng slices, all of the fruit, and the ice cubes into a food processor or blender. Blend on high speed until the fruit is puréed, about 1 minute.

3. Pour into tall glasses and garnish with the mint. Serve immediately.

    NOTE: If you don't have ginseng slices, you can use ginseng tea bags instead.

tropical chocolate fantasy

Among my happiest childhood memories are the rare moments when I savored the rich, velvety flavor of chocolate, a treasured delicacy. To this day, it holds a very special place in my heart. It's hard not to indulge when modern research raves about its antioxidants and other health benefits.

This dessert is another of my East-Meets-West inventions, combining tofu with chocolate chips. Look for dark chocolate chips at health food stores, or use a high-quality dark chocolate bar. Avoid chocolate composed of white sugar, hydrogenated oils, or artificial substances.

MAKES 4 SERVINGS

One 12½-ounce package soft silken tofu

1 large banana, partially frozen for 15 minutes

½ cup honey

1 teaspoon pure vanilla extract

¼ cup semisweet dark chocolate chips

¼ cup sliced almonds, toasted (see page 99)

Small, edible organic flower petals, pesticide-free, for garnish

1. Put the tofu, banana, honey, and vanilla in a blender. Blend on high speed until smooth, about 1 minute. Fold in the chocolate chips.

2. Pour into four parfait or other tall glasses. Cover and refrigerate for 1 hour. Garnish with the almond slices and petal flowers just before serving.

sunrise green tea smoothie

A green tea–fruit smoothie I once had at a spa in California was the inspiration for what is now my favorite morning drink. The myriad health benefits in this smoothie always guard me during flu season. Adjust the number of tea bags based on your desired flavor and amount of caffeine. An average cup (6 ounces) of green tea, brewed with one tea bag, contains about 30 milligrams of caffeine, compared to coffee's 120 milligrams.

MAKES 4 SERVINGS

2 medium bananas, cut into 1-inch slices

4 kiwifruit (about ¾ pound), peeled and cubed

4 fruit-flavored green tea bags

2 cups soy milk

1 tablespoon honey

Fresh or canned cherries, for garnish

1. Place the bananas and kiwifruit in a sealed plastic bag. Freeze for 30 minutes, or until almost firm.

2. Place the tea bags in a medium bowl. Bring the soy milk to a boil. Pour the soy milk over the tea bags and let steep for 3 minutes. Remove the tea bags. Stir in the honey, and set aside to cool.

3. Combine the tea, bananas, and kiwifruit in a blender. Blend on high speed until smooth, about 1 minute. Pour into tall glasses and top with the cherries.

black sesame seed ice cream

During my childhood, I heard about the numerous benefits black sesame provides to women. My grandmother had beautiful, shiny black hair well into her old age. TCM highly praises black sesame, believing that it delays aging, prevents graying hair, regulates digestion, and nourishes the kidneys.

I am always looking for new ways to incorporate it into my diet. When I first tasted black sesame ice cream in the Tokyo airport, I couldn't wait to re-create it at home. I have to admit that ice cream is not my favorite dessert, but this recipe is an exception.

MAKES 6 SERVINGS

2 cups soy creamer or heavy cream

1 cup vanilla soy milk

1 cup creamed hazelnut honey or regular honey

1 cup black sesame seeds, toasted (see page 32)

Fresh mint leaves, for garnish

1. Put the soy creamer, soy milk, honey, and sesame seeds in a blender. Blend on high speed until smooth, about 2 minutes.

2. Transfer the mixture to an ice cream maker. Freeze according to the manufacturer's instructions.

3. Scoop the ice cream into serving dishes. Garnish with the mint and serve immediately.

papaya-soy ice cream

Who says sweet desires have to be loaded with sugar and fat? Here, I've created a nondairy ice cream deriving its flavor from fresh fruit and honey with no refined sugars. Feel free to experiment with other fruits like strawberries, mangoes, or kiwifruit.

You can find whipped toppings made with a tofu base and sweetened with fruit-juice concentrate in the frozen-food section of natural food stores and well-stocked supermarkets.

MAKES 6 SERVINGS

2 small ripe papayas, peeled, seeded, and chopped (about 3 cups)

1 cup vanilla soy milk

½ cup clover honey

2 tablespoons dry coconut flakes

1 cup soy or dairy whipped topping

¼ cup fresh whole raspberries, for garnish

1. Put the papayas, soy milk, honey, and coconut flakes in a blender. Blend on high speed until smooth, about 2 minutes.

2. Transfer the mixture to a metal bowl suitable for freezing. Gently fold the whipped topping into the blended mixture. Cover and freeze for 5 to 6 hours until firm.

3. Scoop the ice cream into serving dishes. Garnish with the raspberries and serve immediately.

NOTE: An easy way to measure out the honey is to first pour the soy milk into a large, demarcated measuring cup. Add honey until the volume has increased by ½ cup. The milk will help keep the honey from sticking to the measuring cup as you pour it into the blender.

For a smoother texture, pour the mixture into an ice cream maker. Freeze according to the manufacturer's instructions.

asian beauty tonic

For centuries, TCM doctors have prescribed red dates, dong quai, and goji berries to regulate hormonal cycles, enhance blood circulation, and beautify the skin. This tonic makes for a delicious, replenishing drink before bedtime during the winter months—an excellent way to end a long, chilly day.

MAKES 4 SERVINGS

4 chai tea bags

2 cups water

2 cups soy milk

8 Chinese dried red dates

4 pieces dried dong quai (see page 000)

4 tablespoons dried goji berries

1. In a large, heavy pot, mix the tea bags, water, soy milk, red dates, dong quai, and goji berries and bring to a boil. Reduce the heat and simmer for 25 to 30 minutes.

2. Remove the tea bags and dong quai. Serve hot. Enjoy the dates and goji berries along with the tonic.

ginger–dong quai chai

When I had a cold as a child, my mother would serve me this ginger chai. Later, in my teen years, she would add dong quai. TCM doctors believe ginger and dong quai replenish the blood supply and improve circulation. Together, they ease menstrual irregularities and balance female hormones. I often serve this at lady's parties in lieu of a punch bowl.

If you aren't going to finish the drink in one serving, leave the tea bags, ginger, and dong quai in the pot to allow their flavors to continue blending.

MAKES 8 SERVINGS

4 chai tea bags or one 16-ounce bottle chai (a mixture of tea and spices, available at most health food stores)

2 cups water

2 cups rice milk

Five ¼-inch slices fresh ginger

4 pieces dried dong quai (see page 5)

Rock sugar or brown sugar

1. In a medium pot, combine the tea bags, water, rice milk, ginger, dong quai, and sugar to taste, and bring to a boil.

2. Reduce the heat and simmer for 8 minutes, or until the rock sugar has dissolved. Discard the tea bags, ginger, and dong quai before serving. Serve hot.

hot pomegranate cider

The unique blend of flavors in this cider makes it an excellent drink for any winter gathering. Goji berries and honey nurture the liver and the digestive system, while cinnamon is a potent tonic for the kidneys' yang.

Modern science suggests that goji berries and cinnamon, as well as cranberries and pomegranates, contain disease-fighting antioxidants. Pomegranates also provide a substantial amount of potassium, as well as vitamin C and niacin.

If you have any cider left over, let it cool, cover, and store it in the refrigerator. It will last for up to four days. Reheat before serving, as it tastes best hot.

MAKES 12 SERVINGS

¼ cup fresh orange peel, cut into 1-inch pieces

3 cinnamon sticks

10 whole cardamom seeds

10 whole cloves

½ gallon (8 cups) pomegranate juice

½ quart (2 cups) apple juice

1 cup water

1 cup honey

2 cups slivered almonds

1 cup dried cranberries

½ cup dried goji berries

1. Wrap the orange peel, cinnamon, cardamom, and cloves in a piece of cheesecloth and tie with kitchen string. In a large pot, combine the pomegranate and apple juices, water, and honey and bring to a boil over medium-high heat.

2. Add the spice bag, cover the pot, and simmer for 10 minutes, stirring occasionally.

3. Stir in the almonds, cranberries, and goji berries and simmer for 10 minutes more. Turn off the heat, remove the spice bag, and ladle the cider into mugs. Serve hot.

steamed asian pears with rock sugar

One winter I told my young son that when I was a little girl in China I would often pretend to have a cough to get my mother to make me rock sugar pears. The next morning, he left me a voice mail: "Mommy, I just wanted to tell you I love you. Cough! Cough-cough. Cough! Can you hear me coughing? I need rock sugar pears." His giggles finished the message as he hung up. How could I deny his request, especially after I had played a similar trick many times on my mother?

Asian pears are also called apple pears because they are crisp, juicy, and round like apples. TCM doctors believe that they have healing properties that soothe the lungs and throat. While steaming, the pears absorb the sugar and become tender. If you don't have rock sugar, substitute it with honey.

MAKES 4 SERVINGS

4 ripe Asian pears

¼ cup rock sugar, broken into very small pieces

Thinly sliced fresh ginger, for garnish

1. Bring water to a boil over high heat in a covered steamer or wok large enough to hold a large steamer rack.

2. Peel the pears. Using a melon baller, working from the top of the pear, remove the stem, core, and seeds. Be careful not to cut through the bottoms of the pears.

3. Fill each hollowed-out pear with 1 tablespoon of rock sugar. Arrange the pears upright in a large bowl.

4. Set the bowl on a steamer rack in the steamer or wok.

5. Cover and steam the pears until they are tender and the rock sugar has melted completely, 15 to 20 minutes.

6. Using oven mitts, carefully lift the lid of the steamer or wok away from you and remove the bowl. Transfer the pears to four small bowls. Garnish each pear with the ginger slices. Serve hot.

citrus fruit cheesecake

Although cheesecake is not an Asian dessert, on a recent visit to Hong Kong, which has strong Western influences, I was served cheesecake made with green tea and fresh fruit. It inspired me to create this East-Meets-West dessert. I flavor the graham cracker crust with lemon zest, but you can choose any citrus flavor. An easy way to crush graham crackers is to place them in a plastic bag and roll over the bag with a rolling pin, or grind them in a blender. You can also purchase graham cracker crumbs.

Powdered pectin is a vegetarian gelling agent. You can usually find it near the gelatin in well-stocked supermarkets. Look for a brand that doesn't require a lot of sugar to gel.

MAKES 8 SERVINGS

crust

1½ cups graham cracker crumbs

¼ cup organic powdered sugar

Grated zest of 1 medium lemon

6 tablespoons (¾ stick) unsalted butter, melted

filling

2 medium grapefruits

2 tablespoons powdered pectin

6 tablespoons organic sugar

1 pound cream cheese

1⅓ cups soy creamer

6 tablespoons orange marmalade

1 tablespoon grated lemon zest

1. Preheat the oven to 350°F (177°C). Lightly coat a 9-inch springform pan with cooking spray.

2. **TO MAKE THE CRUST:** Combine the crumbs, powdered sugar, lemon zest, and butter in a mixing bowl. Mix well. Press the crumb mixture in an even layer on the bottom of the pan. Bake the crust in the oven for 8 to 10 minutes. Transfer to a wire rack to cool.

3. **TO MAKE THE FILLING:** Halve the grapefruits horizontally. Set one half in a bowl, face up, to keep it stable and catch any juices. Cut along both sides of each exposed membrane with a paring knife. Scoop each segment out with a serrated spoon, discarding the membrane. Repeat with the remaining halves. Set aside the grapefruit sections.

4. Combine ¼ cup of the reserved grapefruit juice and the pectin in a small saucepan. Simmer, stirring, over low heat until the pectin dissolves. Set aside and cool to room temperature.

5. Place the pectin-juice mixture, sugar, cream cheese, soy creamer, and orange marmalade in a food processor or blender and blend until smooth. Pour the mixture over the cooled crust and smooth out with a spatula. Cover and refrigerate the cheesecake until set, about 2 hours. Remove the sides of the springform pan. Decorate with the grapefruit sections and lemon zest just before serving.

banana bread pudding with vanilla-rum-chocolate sauce

For years, my sweet comfort food was rice cake, until I tasted banana bread pudding. I love baking this treat while family and friends hover around my kitchen table, chatting excitedly and breathing in the delicious aroma.

I use soy instead of milk to bring an Eastern touch to this classic Western dessert. Black tea accompanies it nicely.

MAKES 6 SERVINGS

bread pudding

3 cups soy milk or rice milk

1 vanilla bean, split lengthwise

½ cup raisins

2 large organic eggs

¼ cup honey

2 large ripe bananas, mashed

3 cups whole wheat bread cubes (about a 1-pound loaf, crusts removed)

½ cup chopped almonds

vanilla-rum-chocolate sauce

½ cup dark soy or regular chocolate chips

2 tablespoons unsalted butter

¼ cup soy creamer

3 tablespoons dark rum

1 teaspoon pure vanilla extract

1. **TO PREPARE THE BREAD PUDDING:** Lightly grease a 9 x 9-inch baking dish. In a medium saucepan, bring the soy milk and vanilla bean to a low boil. Reduce the heat to low and add the raisins. Simmer for 15 minutes.

2. Using tongs, remove the vanilla bean and run the blade of a small knife along the inside of the bean halves to scrape off the seeds. Return the seeds to the milk and discard the vanilla pod (or reserve for another use). Remove the milk from the heat and set aside.

(continued)

3. In a separate bowl, whisk together the eggs, honey, and bananas until well blended. Slowly whisk in the warm milk mixture. Add the bread cubes and stir to moisten thoroughly. Let stand for 10 minutes to allow the bread cubes to absorb the custard. While the mixture stands, preheat the oven to 325°F (163°C).

4. Add the almonds to the pudding mixture and pour into the prepared baking dish. Bake until the edges are golden, 50 minutes to 1 hour.

5. **TO MAKE THE VANILLA-RUM-CHOCOLATE SAUCE:** In a small pot, combine the chocolate chips and butter. Cook, stirring, over low heat until the chocolate chips melt. Stir in the soy creamer, rum, and vanilla. Cut the bread pudding into 6 slices and place on serving plates. Drizzle the chocolate sauce on top. Serve warm.

rice pudding with almonds and coconut

Throughout the world there are endless variations of rice pudding. In this one, I have combined the Middle Eastern version, made with cinnamon and milk, with the Asian style, made with coconut and ginger. The coconut and soy milk combined with crunchy almonds and plump raisins impart richness to this rice pudding. To reduce the fat content, I blend soy milk with coconut milk. This is one of my favorite ways to use leftover cooked rice. For an even healthier version, I use sweet brown rice.

MAKES 6 TO 8 SERVINGS

1 cup cooked sweet brown rice

2 teaspoons minced fresh ginger

6 cups soy milk

2 cups reduced-fat, unsweetened coconut milk

½ teaspoon ground cinnamon

Honey

⅓ cup sliced almonds, toasted (see page 99)

½ cup golden raisins

1. Put the rice, ginger, and soy milk in a large pot and bring to a boil. Reduce the heat to low, partially cover the pan, and simmer, stirring occasionally, for 40 minutes.

2. Stir in the coconut milk, cinnamon, and honey. Simmer until the pudding develops a thick porridge-like consistency, about 10 minutes.

3. Top with the almonds and raisins. Serve warm or cold.

sweet eight-treasure rice pudding

Eight-treasure rice pudding is a well-known Chinese dessert traditionally served at banquets. Its name comes from the jewel-like appearance of eight different types of fresh or dried fruits and nuts cooked with rice. Once steamed, the dried fruits become plump and soft, releasing their delightful sweetness.

Despite the name, people today rarely cook it with the eight treasures, so don't feel cheated that this recipe only contains five. The "jewels" depend on the seasons and vary by region. Feel free to substitute different fruits and nuts to your liking, or whatever you have on hand. My son likes to throw in a handful of chocolate chips.

MAKES 4 SERVINGS

½ cup chopped fresh mango

¼ cup fresh, seedless green grapes, halved or quartered

¼ cup dried tart cherries

¼ cup golden raisins

¼ cup chopped candied pineapple

1 cup cooked glutinous rice

½ cup almond or peanut butter

¼ cup pure maple syrup

1. Line the bottom of an 8-inch bowl with plastic wrap. Attractively arrange the mango, grapes, cherries, raisins, and pineapple on the bottom of the lined bowl.

2. Pack half of the warm rice on top of the fruit in an even layer, following the curve of the bowl. Spread the almond butter and syrup over the rice.

3. Pack the remaining rice over the almond butter–syrup layer. Flatten the top of the rice firmly.

4. Place a platter on top of the bowl and invert, holding them together. Lift off the bowl and remove the plastic wrap to reveal the beautifully arranged fruit treasures. Serve warm.

new year's rice cake

Just as American children anxiously await their Christmas gifts months in advance, I anxiously awaited this scrumptious cake.

Nian-Gao, New Year's cake, is one of the most important holiday dishes in many Asian countries. Eating Nian-Gao during the New Year's celebration is said to bring safety and fortune to the entire family for the coming year, though I now make it for family gatherings throughout the year.

MAKES 8 SERVINGS

1 pound glutinous rice flour (also called sweet rice flour)

1¼ cups sugar

1 tablespoon baking powder

¼ cup dried cherries

¼ cup chopped candied pineapple

¼ cup dried dates

¼ cup chopped nuts

3 large organic eggs

¾ cup extra-virgin olive oil

1½ cups water

Raisins, nuts, and dried cherries, for decoration

1. Preheat the oven to 375°F (191°C). Coat a 9-inch round cake pan with non-stick cooking spray.

2. Combine the rice flour, sugar, baking powder, cherries, pineapple, dates, and nuts in a large mixing bowl. Mix to combine thoroughly.

3. In a separate bowl, beat the eggs. Add the oil and water to the eggs and whisk to blend well. Pour the egg mixture into the fruit mixture and mix thoroughly.

4. Pour the batter into the prepared pan. Bake for 40 minutes, or until a knife inserted into the center comes out clean. The cake will have risen when done.

5. To remove the cake from the pan, place a serving plate over the cake pan. Holding the plate and the pan together, invert and give the pan a little shake; the cake should drop out onto the plate.

6. Decorate the cake with three raisins each for eyes, nuts for the nose, and cherries for a smile. Serve warm.

jasmine tea almond cookies

Almond cookies are a quintessential Chinese dessert. I modified them by adding jasmine tea, which lends the cookies a subtle, fresh flavor, making them a delicious finale to a hearty meal.

On warm days, I serve them with frozen yogurt or fresh fruit. Once the cookies have cooled, store them in a tightly sealed container. They will last for up to five days.

MAKES 40 COOKIES

¾ cup all-purpose flour

Contents of 3 jasmine green tea bags

½ teaspoon baking soda

⅛ teaspoon salt

¼ cup plus 2 tablespoons unsalted butter (or vegan margarine)

¼ cup almond butter

½ cup plus 2 tablespoons organic milled golden cane sugar

1 large organic egg, lightly beaten

1 teaspoon pure vanilla extract

40 unblanched whole almonds

1. Preheat the oven to 350°F. Lightly spray two baking sheets with nonstick cooking spray.

2. In a medium bowl, combine the flour, tea, baking soda, and salt. Set aside.

3. In a large, ovenproof bowl, combine the butter and almond butter. Place in the oven for 3 to 5 minutes to soften the butter.

4. Add the sugar to the butter and almond butter. Mix with a wooden spoon until light and fluffy, then beat in the egg and vanilla until blended. Add the egg mixture to the flour mixture and beat until combined.

5. Spray a ½-tablespoon measuring spoon with nonstick cooking spray. Spoon balls of the dough onto the prepared baking sheets, spacing them about 2 inches apart. Press an almond into the top of each ball.

6. Bake for 13 to 15 minutes, or until the cookies are lightly browned. Transfer to a rack to cool completely.

INDEX

Note: Page references in *italics* refer to photographs.